How to
Speak
in Church

How to Speak in Church

Emerson Roy West

Published by
Deseret Book Company
Salt Lake City, Utah
1976

To my wife,
Gloria,
who is my
inspiration
in life,
and to
my children,
Jerry,
Jennifer,
Julie Ann,
and Janelle

Contents

Acknowledgments

Grateful acknowledgment is given to all who contributed to the reality of this book, including family, friends, teachers, colleagues, and students. Particular appreciation is extended to the following:

Nancy Wudel, for her inspiration and excellent editorial assistance.

Roy A. West, my father, who played an important role in the development of the book.

Golden K. Driggs, for his interest, suggestions, and constant encouragement.

Royal L. Garff, professor of speech, for his critical analysis of the speech principles and for offering helpful suggestions.

Wm. James Mortimer and his staff at Deseret Book for inspiration, encouragement, and professional help.

Keith Montague and associates for the design and artwork.

Dr. Harold Glen Clark, Dr. Robert J. Matthews, Dr. J. LaVar Bateman, Dr. Roy W. Doxey, Dr. Joseph C. Muren, Horace J. Ritchie, Leonard C. Smith, Mary Bradford, Nancy Wilson, and Patricia Tate for many helpful suggestions.

And last but certainly not least, my wonderful companion, Gloria, for her constant support, counsel, research, evaluating, encouragement, and splendid secretarial service in typing the manuscript.

Appreciation is also extended to authors and publishers who have granted permission to use their material.

Preface

One of the exciting rewards of membership in The Church of Jesus Christ of Latter-day Saints can be delivering a talk in church successfully. However, some members dread speaking opportunities because they lack the know-how or ability that gives them the confidence to enjoy public speaking.

Basically, the rules that govern effective public speaking apply also to speaking in church. The purpose of this book, therefore, is to take good public speaking principles and apply them specifically to church speaking, to help make the experience more enjoyable and less frightening.

While no formula for public speaking guarantees a successful presentation every time one speaks, the possibilities of failure can certainly be reduced. If Latter-day Saints will thoughtfully read these chapters and begin practicing the principles discussed herein, they will find their speaking ability greatly improved and their confidence "waxing strong."

Jesus said, "If ye know these things, happy are ye if ye do them." (John 13:17.) Every speaker should "know these things" if he sincerely desires to inspire his audience and uplift himself.

CHAPTER 1

Why Speak in Church

Two missionaries sat near the rear of the chapel. Beside them was an investigator, a sincere woman with pensive yet questioning lines marking her brow. Her life had been void of gospel truths, and now she searched and studied for life's purposes.

The assigned speaker arose and began his sermon. As he spoke, he unfolded a story that struck responsive chords within the woman—at first exhibited in teary blinks, then gentle teardrops, and finally quiet sobs.

As the speaker concluded, the woman turned to the missionaries and, through joyful tears, explained, "He spoke about a subject tender to me. He answered a question that has troubled me for years. I have received the final link I have been searching for, and I am now ready for baptism."

This experience, which took place not long ago in Rochester, Minnesota, is only one of hundreds of penetrating stories illustrating the great power and importance of speaking in church.

The Savior himself used the medium of public speaking to teach some of his most beautiful precepts, as he delivered the Sermon on the Mount and preached to the multitudes. In one of the most profound admonitions of latter-day scripture, he said, "And verily I say unto thee that thou shalt lay aside the things of this world, and seek for the things of a better." (D&C 25:10.)

In that simple command lies much meaning and purpose for life, and therein lies a major purpose of church speaking. The call to speak in church is the call to win souls for Jesus Christ and to help them seek for the things of a better world.

On one occasion the Lord said:

And I give you a commandment that you shall teach one another the doctrine of the kingdom.

Teach ye diligently and my grace shall attend you, that you may be instructed more perfectly in theory, in principle, in doctrine, in the law of the gospel, in all things that pertain unto the kingdom of God, that are expedient for you to understand. (D&C 88:77-78.)

Preaching has been part of the gospel order from the beginning. After naming the great patriarchs from Adam to Enoch, Moses commented: "And they were preachers of righteousness, and spake and prophesied, and called upon all men everywhere, to repent; and faith was taught unto the children of men." (Moses 6:23.)

The prophet Mormon told of a short speech directed to him when he was about ten years old that set the pattern for his entire life. (See Mormon 1:2-5.)

Perhaps speech was never more effectively used in teaching than when it was used by the Father and Son in the Sacred Grove in the spring of 1820, when they spoke to the fourteen-year-old Joseph Smith. As Joseph became a prophet of God, he too used the powerful tool of speech to eloquently instruct, uplift, and motivate.

Church history is replete with examples that clearly show that people need to be told continually that life does have a purpose and that they have a duty. There is a power, a spirit, a stimulation that comes as people hear words of truth.

Church speaking can provide valuable input for our mental and spiritual well-being. It has the potential to be highly nutritional spiritual food to the soul. But just as physical food can be improved in flavor and nutritional value by seasoning and proper preparation, so spiritual food can be served at its highest degree of excellence through the proper preparations.

Frequently one hears this comment: "That was one of the best sacrament meetings we have ever had." What is really meant is

2

probably "I was spiritually fed tonight." By learning how to prepare and serve spiritual food, Church members can be much better speakers and teachers of the "doctrine of the kingdom." (D&C 88:77.)

The preacher Billy Sunday once said, "Going to church on Sunday no more makes you a Christian than sleeping in the garage makes you a car." And so it is with church speaking. One cannot expect to stand and deliver a masterpiece without the necessary preparations of knowledge and the daily preparations with the Lord.

Successful church speaking accomplishes three purposes:

1. It captures the listener's interest as it challenges and persuades.

2. It communicates gospel messages that build faith and testimony.

3. It inspires the listener with desire and courage to apply the message to his daily living.

Formal pulpit speaking may, in fact, help solve important problems dealing with the spiritual, temporal, and moral welfare of the listeners, as with the woman in Minnesota. A gospel message from the pulpit can inspire hope, repentance, and rededication. It can rekindle appreciation and faith.

Paul's solemn charge to Timothy was: "Preach the word; be instant in season, out of season; reprove, rebuke, exhort with all longsuffering and doctrine." (2 Timothy 4:2.)

The primary aim of church speaking is simple: to preach the word of God. If this is the overall quest, the three specific purposes mentioned will indeed be accomplished. The speaker will stand before a congregation that experiences all the mingled feelings from the spectrum of life—and he will bring light. He will radiate an aura of help and uplifting. He will move his listeners Godward as he motivates them to truly seek for the things of a better world.

CHAPTER 2

The
Speaker

Of all the truths in the Bible, one of the most profound is the statement of the Savior to Peter, "Thy speech bewrayeth thee." (See Matthew 26:73.) The word *bewray*, an archaic term not used today, means "reveal," and certainly one's speech does reveal much about him.

Effective Church speakers have learned that "out of the abundance of the heart the mouth speaketh." (Matthew 12:34.) The call to be a speaker is not just a call for speaking, but for living. Before one can develop good speaking skills and techniques, he should first develop the essential qualities for good living, such as sincerity, honesty, and humility.

The more sincere a speaker is and the more diligently he tries to live as he speaks, the more impact his words will have on his audience. A master teacher is one whose living ability has caught up with his speaking ability.

Perhaps one of the most encouraging stories of the scriptures is that of the Lord's calling Enoch to be a prophet. When Enoch received the call, he "bowed himself to the earth" and asked the Lord, "Why is it that I have found favor in thy sight, and am but a lad, and all the people hate me; for I am slow of speech; wherefore am I thy servant?"

And the Lord said to him, "Go forth and do as I have commanded thee. . . . Open thy mouth, and it shall be filled. . . . therefore walk with me." (Moses 6:31-34.)

Enoch did just that, and he came to be one of God's noblest prophets. The formula the Lord gave to Enoch—"walk with me"—can apply just as directly to each member of the Church. As we follow the steps of prayer, study, and obedience, we receive spiritual strength and confidence that will reflect in our speech presentation.

The Savior has given us the power of his example in public speaking as well as in his manner of living. "Master, teach us" was the plea of those gathered at his feet to learn wisdom and knowledge. He had a powerful gift for speaking because he himself lived the precepts of which he spoke. He knew his subject; he understood the needs of his audience; and he lived what he spoke. And so the people flocked to hear him speak.

As you begin your task of becoming a better church speaker, then, you must first begin developing those ideal personal characteristics epitomized by the Savior. Among these characteristics are the following:

1. Believe in yourself.

"Success or failure in a business is caused more by mental attitudes than by mental capacities," said Walter Dill Scott. Substitute "church speaking" for the word *business*, and the sentence now reads: "Success or failure in *church speaking* is caused more by mental attitudes than by mental capacities." The person called to speak must believe in himself.

Some people have immediate negative reactions when they are called to speak. Into their minds come thoughts of fear, failure, or defeat. The familiar cries of "I'm just not a speaker," "I'm not worthy," or "I'm too frightened" will probably be felt by the audience if you are poorly prepared and lack confidence and faith.

Church members should therefore condition themselves to have an immediate positive reaction when called upon to speak and to welcome the opportunity. Their reaction should be, "If God be for us, who can be against us?" (Romans 8:31.) Train yourself to fill your mind with thoughts of faith, confidence, and security. If you repeatedly say to yourself, "I can do all things through Christ which strengtheneth me" (Philippians 4:13), how uplifting and positive will be the vibrations felt by those who hear you speak!

5

2. Be prepared.

Preparation is one of the most important requirements of the good speaker, just as it is of the good teacher. President David O. McKay once said to a missionary class, "Preparation precedes power." If you talk for fifteen minutes to a congregation of 250 people, you are responsible for more than sixty individual hours of influencing lives. In such a gospel setting, each minute to each person can be eternally valuable. Thus, you have a vast responsibility with each minute you speak.

Jesus himself lived upon the earth only thirty-three years, but thirty of those years were spent in preparing for his earthly ministry, which formally lasted only three years. The scriptures are filled with admonitions to prepare, such as, "Prepare yourselves for that which is to come" and "Prepare your hearts."

A speech is like a house: a house cannot be built without a blueprint, and a successful speech cannot be presented without a written plan. Jesus said, ". . . if ye are prepared, ye shall not fear." (D&C 38:30.)

3. Learn to pray.

It has been said that "he who would speak to man for God, must speak much to God for man." A prayerless speaker or person is powerless and profitless. Much prayer equals much power, while little prayer equals little power.

Prayer is vital for giving one peace, confidence, and the ability to reach the needs of the audience. We have been told, "Counsel with the Lord in all thy doings." (Alma 37:37.) Considering the great responsibility given to a speaker, counseling with the Lord is the only sure way to select the proper subject, message, and material.

Soon after you are called to speak, seek strength and guidance from the Lord. As you prepare, consult with him often through prayer and seek confirmation that your message is indeed that which the Lord would have you present.

Two missionaries who had an appointment to teach the gospel to a school group prepared diligently and were confident the Spirit would help them. Then they met with the group at the appointed time and delivered their message. But to their distress, the meeting was devoid of a spiritual uplift, and they left it confused and disappointed. When they later told their mission president what had happened, he asked, "Did you get on your knees before leaving for the meeting and invite the Holy Ghost to be there?"

The elders shook their heads. The mission president continued, "Would you ever go to a gathering uninvited? Well, neither would the Holy Ghost. If you want him to be there, you must invite him."

The missionaries learned never to assume that the Spirit would automatically be with them in their work.

Jesus himself lived a life of prayer and admonished that men ought to pray always and not faint. Therefore, ask yourself: Do I pray often? Do I find a secret place and pray aloud? Do I talk with God as with a father and friend? Do I counsel with him in all my doings? Have I told him my needs and desires in preparing and delivering my talk?

4. Study the gospel.

The teacher of any subject must have a basic knowledge of his subject. As obvious as that statement might seem, it is still an important one to remember in preparing for speaking in church. A mathematics teacher must know mathematics; a music teacher, music; a Spanish teacher, Spanish. Likewise, a gospel teacher must know the basics of the gospel.

Knowledge is not inherited—it must be learned. No one knows anything about his homeland simply because he was born there. And in like manner, no one knows anything about Christ's work simply because he is a member of the Church. He must consistently study and learn about the gospel.

Dr. John A. Widtsoe, a former member of the Council of the Twelve, university president, and scientist, in his autobiography *In a Sunlit Land*, described his preparation for the apostleship:

I had studied the gospel as carefully as any science. The literature of the Church I had acquired and read. During my spare time, day by day, I had increased my gospel learning. . . .

The claims of Joseph Smith the Prophet had been examined and weighed. No scientific claim had received a more thorough analysis. (Deseret Book, 1953, p. 158.)

7

Through knowledge, prayer, and preparation comes speaking power.

5. Develop Christlike love.

The first and great commandment to all speakers of the gospel is: "Thou shalt love the Lord thy God with all thy heart, and with all thy soul, and with all thy mind." (Matthew 22:37.) We might paraphrase the second great commandment, which is like unto it: "Thou shalt love thy audience as thyself." (See Matthew 22:39.) On these two charges hangs a key to effective speaking.

Listeners can sense the spirit of love radiating from a speaker. The gospel cannot be spoken or preached in righteousness without "love unfeigned." (See D&C 121:41.) It is difficult to deliver an inspiring message without deep love for and desire to help the audience. Remember the example of love that Christ had for those to whom he spoke. He had compassion for the blind in their darkness (Matthew 20:34); for the lepers in their uncleanness (Mark 14:14); for the hungry in their need (Matthew 15:32); for the friendless in their loneliness (Mark 6:34); and for those who were sorrowing (Luke 7:1). The speaker who really loves people will make the necessary preparations to inspire them. Nowhere does the Lord say, "If you love me, tell me." He says, in essence, "If ye love me, *show* me. Keep my commandments."

In a speaking assignment one may show his love to the Lord and his fellowmen by diligently preparing and drawing the Holy Ghost to us. In that way he may be able to help his listeners draw closer to the Lord.

6. Learn obedience.

A college coed in the process of making a decision regarding her marriage partner had gone through much emotional turmoil and indecision, so she had decided to fast one Sunday to seek for divine help and direction. She began her fast, attended Sunday School, and then came home to do her school homework. When her roommates offered her a ride to sacrament meeting, she said, "Oh, I just can't go. I have to finish this term paper. It's due tomorrow." Yet, she continued fasting for an answer to her problem.

Here was a girl who did not understand the principle of obedience. She wanted divine help, but she didn't do her part to receive that blessing. One cannot expect help with his church assignments when he doesn't do his part and keep the commandments. The Spirit must flow through a channel of righteous desires. Each speaker might well adopt this prayer: "Create in me a clean heart, O God; and renew a right spirit within me." (Psalm 51:10.)

7. Seek for gifts of the Spirit.

Gifts of the Spirit are bestowed upon men when they show their worthiness to receive these gifts through their devotion, faith, and obedience. The Lord has said, "And when we obtain any blessing from God, it is by obedience to that law upon which it is predicated." (D&C 130:21.) In Moroni we learn that gifts of the Spirit "come by the Spirit of Christ," that "every good gift cometh of Christ." (See Moroni 10:17-18.) The spirit, or light, of Christ is the agency through which the Holy Ghost operates.

Seek the direction of the Holy Ghost, for his mission is to convince, convert, comfort, inspire, correct, and instruct on righteousness. Prepare yourself to be worthy to have the help of the Holy Ghost in your study, planning, and delivery. Under his influence, you can be led to choose the right subject, and members of the audience can be unified and their hearts opened to the message you wish to present. We have been told that all faithful Saints have the right to gifts of the Spirit and that such gifts are necessary for our perfection, but we must ask for them.

Of course, part of asking is listening. Learn to pause and listen for the promptings of the Spirit. President McKay related a story concerning the wife of Bishop John Wells, former member of the Presiding Bishopric, who was heartbroken at the accidental death of her son. She was not consoled until one day when, as she was lying on her bed, her son appeared to her and explained the circumstances surrounding his death. Then the son explained that he had tried to see his father, but his father had been so busy with church duties that he could not respond to his call, so he had come to his mother. He said to her, "You tell father that all is well with me, and I want you not to mourn anymore."

To get the gifts of the Spirit, seek for them and then put yourself in a situation and state of mind to receive them.

8. Be humble.

Many uplifting sermons have been delivered through true humility. A speaker's natural speaking ability may be weak but his spirit of humility can be so impressive and touching that the audience is moved. Many church members misunderstand what humility really is. It does not mean weaknesses, or speaking low, or mediocrity. Humility denotes spiritual strength and clear speaking and thinking. It is not so much a way of speaking as an attitude and feeling while speaking. A speaker who exhibits humility is one who radiates sincere appreciation and recognition of the Lord for his blessings.

Some Don'ts for Speakers

Here are some considerations to which the church speaker might well give heed:

1. Be careful not to give a false impression of great intellect or culture. Don't flaunt your knowledge or accomplishments.

2. Be as aware of your strengths as your weaknesses. It is often one's strengths that cause him to be overconfident.

3. Beware of pride, which is one of the deadliest and the most subtle of all sins in public speaking. Be natural in the things you do, and avoid a false appearance of piety or self-righteousness.

The Savior's Example

To summarize the qualities of a good speaker, let's look again at the Savior's example. He had power of conviction because of his great knowledge of the gospel. He knew the needs and the problems of his listeners. He loved all people even when he disapproved of what they did. He radiated enthusiasm for his message, which made his listeners enthusiastic about the truths of which he spoke. He was friendly and had an extremely approachable manner. He touched the hearts and souls of those who heard him.

Remember also the great examples of the sons of Mosiah, who were very successful speakers and teachers. In the Book of Mormon, it is recorded:

. . . *yea, and they had waxed strong in the knowledge of the truth; for they were men of a sound understanding and they had searched the scriptures diligently, that they might know the word of God.*

10

But this is not all; they had given themselves to much prayer, and fasting; therefore they had the spirit of prophecy, and the spirit of revelation, and when they taught, they taught with power and authority of God. (Alma 17:2-3.)

A speaker cannot communicate conviction without paying the price for conviction for himself. Neither can a speaker touch hearts without the Spirit of the Lord. Those desiring to improve their speaking ability should take to heart the admonition of the Savior when he said, "Follow me."

CHAPTER 3

The Audience

Whether it was in the market-place or on the mountain slope, Jesus always had an audience. Wherever he went, he was surrounded by congregations who wanted to hear his words. People thronged around him because in him they found a friend, someone who understood their needs and their desires. They had great confidence in his ability to help them.

Jesus is the prime example of a speaker who empathized with his audience. He was moved to compassion by all whom he met and felt their problems as his own. He was not preoccupied with the masses—his concern was the one. As he spoke to the crowd, he singled out the individual. He noticed Zacchaeus and was aware of both his needs and his future potentialities. He spoke specifically to Peter, James, and John, was aware of the blind beggar by the roadside, spoke kindly to Mary Magdalene, and talked with the woman by the well.

The way a speaker views his audience influences his attitude, the content of his message, and even the tone of his voice. How he sees his audience is determined by his own understanding, compassion, and insight into human differences and needs.

As you begin expanding your speaking talents, the challenge is to learn to understand your audience and how to relate to them. No matter how valuable your ideas, no matter how great your enthusiasm, your message will not be fully accepted if your thoughts and your manner of delivery are not adapted to the level of understanding of the people you are addressing. A good speech is never merely a general statement addressed "To whom it may concern." It has as much individuality as a personal letter. Learn therefore to adjust your message to your audience. Know something about their nature and needs. It may be assumed that all listeners have certain general spiritual needs—to repent, to believe, to pray, to love, to serve, to grow, to study the scriptures. How can you try to help meet those needs?

Let's look at the individual differences and individual types of people often present in one type of audience—a ward sacrament meeting congregation. Individual differences might include:

1. Church experience and training
2. Formal educational background
3. Emotional maturity and development
4. Age
5. Mental ability
6. Status of health
7. Sex
8. Family background
9. Marital status
10. Ambitions and goals

A speaker must recognize and respond to these differences if he is to hold interest and obtain the response he desires. A typical audience might be composed of the following general types of people:

1. *Children,* who are forming attitudes toward life and religion and are very impressionable. They have a short interest span, so it is good to use lively, visual words frequently.

2. *Teenagers,* who are in a period of transition, beset with decision-making and sometimes confusion. Many of life's permanent choices are made during this period, often without guidance or help. To help them, present ideas that are sound and clear, always be sincere, and avoid talking down to them.

3. *Young adults,* whose lives are busy and who may be attempting to establish themselves in professions or who may be immersed in educational pursuits. They are striving to get ahead, to meet deadlines, to make payments on a house or car. They may be

experiencing one of life's greatest responsibilities, parenthood. All these activities bring a new dimension to life—and new problems.

4. *Middle-aged persons*, for whom this is a time of growth, increasing success, and significant achievement. For some it is also a time of disillusionment; they have not attained the positions they desired, and they recognize that some of their youthful ambitions may not be realized. Perhaps their children have become more of a problem than a pleasure. A church speaker can help provide revitalization for those in this group.

5. *Elderly persons*, who may number more than 10 percent of the members of the congregation. These people also have problems. Their families may be far away, or they may have serious economic, personal, or emotional problems. Housing, limited income, loss of friends, loss of prestige, failing health—all these are problems with which they may have to cope.

6. *Investigators*. Since ours is a missionary church, nonmembers may be present. Talk simply about gospel truths, never criticize other churches, and stick to basic gospel doctrine.

7. *Persons who are single, widowed, or divorced.* These people often have special concerns and sorrows, and may need to have their faith renewed and an assurance that they are important.

8. *Part-member families.* Common to every congregation are husbands or wives who attend meetings alone, without the companionship and support of their partner. To this group, send out messages of hope, encouragement, and love.

Of all the age group categories, probably the children and the older people are most neglected in church speaking. One older person asked a ward bishop, "What about us? Speakers in the ward spend much time speaking to the young people and to young parents, and well they should; but is it asking too much for speakers to think, plan, speak, and pray in terms of older people?" She spoke about some specific needs of older people. "We prefer talks that deal with peace, comfort, patience, the constructive use of conflict, pain, suffering, spiritual growth, adjustments to losses, sorrow, anxiety, disability, prayer, and the four truths that abide eternally—faith, hope, love, and resurrection."

As you examine the makeup of your audience, you may feel confused by the diversity of needs. However, as you become aware

14

of these persons and exercise prayer in your preparation, you will find that the task is not so difficult. The Holy Ghost is the catalyst that gives a message universal appeal. The parables of the Savior held messages for the uneducated as well as the intellectual, the young as well as the old. So it is when one speaks with the influence of the Holy Ghost. As you speak simply and clearly, the Spirit can send the message into the hearts of all.

After you have analyzed your audience's needs and interests, analyze your own ability to make your message applicable to their lives. A sermon or speech without application to life is of no value. Application means to put to use. One speaker made this observation: "A person speaking in church without making an application would be like a physician giving his patient a lecture on general health and forgetting to write out a much-needed prescription." The application, therefore, is a vital part of the sermon or talk, because it is the part that motivates the listener to action. Without it, the sermon may fail.

King Benjamin, a prophet-king of the Nephite nation and one of the powerful speakers of the Book of Mormon, understood the importance of application in speaking. Some of the important points in his great sermon to the nation are:

1. The value of serving one's fellowmen. (Mosiah 2:11-21.)

2. The value of keeping God's commandments. (Mosiah 2:22-24, 41.)

3. A warning against transgression. (Mosiah 2:32-40.)

4. The importance of Christ's mission—the atonement. (Mosiah 3:5-27.)

5. The principle upon which salvation is based—trust in God and obedience to his commandments. (Mosiah 4:6-30.)

He gave his listeners something they could apply in their lives. What effect did the sermon have upon them? Did they take the message with a desire to apply it to their lives? The answer can only be yes, because the sermon produced humility and repentance (Mosiah 4:1-2), created a desire in them to change their manner of living, and caused them to enter into a covenant to keep God's commandments (Mosiah 5:1-8).

15

When asked if they believed the words that Benjamin had spoken,

they all cried with one voice, saying: Yea, we believe all the words which thou hast spoken unto us; and also, we know of their surety and truth, because of the Spirit of the Lord Omnipotent, which has wrought a mighty change in us, or in our hearts, that we have no more disposition to do evil, but to do good continually. (Mosiah 5:2.)

A Latter-day Saint who attended a sacrament meeting in a distant city during a business trip congratulated the high councilor for his sermon. "But," said the businessman, "if you were my salesman I'd discharge you. You got my attention by your appearance, your voice, and your manner, and the organization of your speech aroused my interest. In fact, you warmed my heart with a desire to do what you said, but then you stopped without asking me to do something about it. In business, the important thing is to get your contact to sign on the dotted line."

It is essential to give listeners something to take home—an idea, a thought, or a plan for better living, but always something that will apply to their lives.

To summarize, first analyze the audience and understand their situations and needs. Consider the many problems they may have, and realize that many difficult situations are brought about because of change in life style, residence, employment, ethics, morality. Your duty, as a speaker, is to help bring stability and spiritual strength amid the changes in life.

Second, consider the best means of applying the message to the audience in view of their particular needs. Always conclude your presentation with a challenge, thought, idea, or plan of action that will help them put your words into action.

And third, remember that there are those in the audience who are waiting for you to say something that will give assurance, hope, courage, power, and faith. Herein lies the supreme significance of the talk in church.

CHAPTER 4

Selecting Your Subject

For many who are called to speak, the talk itself is not so harrowing an experience as choosing the subject about which to speak. Some speakers try to solve the problem by avoiding it—they never do choose one particular topic. Like a disorganized gardener, they pull out a few radishes, then some carrots, and then start picking beans, never completing any one task.

The effective speaker finds that a spiritual feast is best accomplished when he has focused upon one specific message and purpose. The first questions of a person who has been asked to speak usually are "What shall I talk about?" and "Where do I start?"

The first step is one that some speakers overlook—the step of spiritual preparation. This is the place to start, with earnest, humble prayer for divine guidance and inspiration. The Lord has said, "Be thou humble; and the Lord thy God shall lead thee by the hand, and give thee answer to thy prayers." (D&C 112:10.)

So begin humbly, believingly, and with faith. The speaker who immediately reacts to a speaking assignment with the thoughts: "I knew they would realize what I have to offer" or "Wait until they hear my talk, I'll really set them on fire," will probably find his talk devoid of spiritual support. On the other hand, the speaker who acknowledges his dependence on the Lord and who conscientiously studies and prays is the speaker who will have a successful speaking experience.

After you have taken the time to think about a possible subject, ask the Lord in prayer for guidance. He has said, "But, behold, I say unto you, that you must study it out in your mind; then you must ask me if it be right, and if it is right I will cause that your bosom shall burn within you; therefore, you shall feel that it is right." (D&C 9:8.)

After spiritual preparation, begin searching for subject ideas.

1.   Choose a topic that you are familiar with, one in which you are interested and about which you can share personal feelings and testimony.

2.   Choose a subject of present interest, one in harmony with the occasion.

3.   Choose a subject that you truly believe in and about which you have a burning testimony. Nothing rings more clearly to a congregation than the tones of hypocrisy.

4.   Consider the intelligence of the congregation and choose a subject suited to them, not a highly intellectual topic or one that will be over their heads.

5.   Avoid a theme that is controversial or deals with speculation and sensationalism.

6.   Train your mind to be sensitive to ideas that might be developed into talks. An idea might come from a scripture, general conference talk, Sunday School lesson, current event, or seasonal celebration.

After you have some ideas, choose a general subject and begin narrowing it down to a specific topic. Sometimes speakers run into trouble because they settle on a subject that is too broad to handle. For example, no speaker could discuss the complete subject of faith in ten or twenty minutes. First select a subject and then draw from this subject a specific topic. The message should be plain, clear, and brief, with a definite aim and unity of thought. The process of limiting a subject through the use of topics may be seen in the following example.

A member was recently asked to speak in sacrament meeting. After much contemplation and prayer, he selected the subject of faith. Now his task was to limit the subject to a specific topic that could be covered in the allotted time, so he sat down with a piece of paper and a pencil and listed possible topics, such as:

18

1. Faith in action
2. Attributes of faith
3. Faith and belief
4. Faith and the commandments
5. Faith for creative living
6. The meaning of faith in Christ
7. Faith, the principle of progress
8. Faith and prayers
9. Faith and works
10. Faith and testimony
11. The power of faith
12. How faith grows

After prayerful consideration, he decided to speak about faith in action. He felt confident that he could share some helpful thoughts on that subject, his personal testimony, and some heart-warming personal experiences. After he made this decision, he went to the Lord for confirmation and then began to prepare his talk.

Briefly, then, the process of choosing a subject and message is, first, prepare spiritually; second, gather ideas; third, choose a subject; fourth, narrow the field and choose a specific topic; and fifth, seek divine confirmation.

The process of selecting the topic can be as rewarding and uplifting as the actual delivery if you seek divine guidance and remember your foremost responsibility in speaking in church—to inspire and help "bring to pass the immortality and eternal life of man." (See Moses 1:39.)

Following is a list of subjects that may lend themselves to successful, inspirational church talks. Read through the list and then begin thinking about those with which you already have some familiarity.

Possible Subjects for Church Talks

Aaronic Priesthood	Athletics	Baptism for the dead
America	Attitude	Behavior
Angels	Atonement	Belief
Apostasy	Authority	Bible
Apostles	Baptism	Blessings

19

Book of Mormon
Book of remembrance
Brotherhood
Careers
Caring
Celestial kingdom
Character
Charity
Chastity
Children
Christ, Jesus
Christianity
Christmas
Church activity
Church callings
Church government
Church growth
Church history
Church leaders
Church and its mission
Church organization
Citizenship
Commandments
Commitment
Common consent
Communication
Compassion
Consecration
Conversion
Courage
Covenants
Creation
Crucifixion
Dating
Death
Decisions
Degrees of glory
Discipleship

Dispensations
Doctrine and Covenants
Doctrines
Duty
Earth life
Easter
Education
Endowments
Eternal increase
Eternal life
Eternal principles
Eternal progression
Evil
Exaltation
Example
Faith
Fall of man
Family
Family home evening
Fasting
Fast offering
Fathers
Fault-finding
Fellowship
Finances
Food storage
Foreordination
Forgiveness
Free agency
Freedom
Friends
Gathering of Israel
Genealogy
General Authorities
Gifts of Spirit
Giving
Goals
God

Good and evil
Good works
Gospel
Gossip
Government
Habits
Happiness
Healings
Health
Heaven
Heritage
Holy Ghost
Holy Spirit
Home
Honesty
Ideals
Immorality
Immortality
Inactivity
Individuality
Integrity
Intelligence
Israel
Joy
Judgment
Justice
Keys of the
  kingdom
Kindness
Kingdom of God
Knowledge
Lamanites
Last days
Last dispensation
Law
Leadership
Life

Light of Christ
Love
Loyalty
Man
Marriage
Melchizedek
   Priesthood
Mercy
Millennium
Miracles
Missionary work
Modesty
Money
Morality
Mormonism
Mortality
Mothers
Music
Obedience
Opposition
Ordinances
Parents
Patriarchal blessing
Patriarchal order
Patriarchs
Patriotism
Peace
Pearl of Great Price
Perfection
Physical fitness
Pioneers
Preparation
Presidents
   of the Church
Priesthood
Primary
Profanity
Prophets

Prophecy
Reactivation
Recreation
Redemption
Religion
Religious education
Repentance
Responsibility
Restoration
Resurrection
Relief Society
Revelation
Reverence
Rewards
Righteousness
Sabbath day
Sacrament
Sacrifice
Salvation
Satan
Scouting
Scriptures
Second coming of Christ
Self-control
Self-worth
Service
Sexual morality
Signs of the times
Sin
Singular life, the
Sorrow
Speech
Spirit world
Spirit of God
Spiritual death
Spiritual gifts
Spirituality
Standards

Stewardship
Storage plan
Success
Succession in the
   Presidency
Sunday School
Suffering
Teaching
Telestial kingdom
Temples
Temptation
Terrestrial kingdom
Testimony
Thanksgiving
Thrift
Tithing
Tolerance
Transfiguration
Trials
Truth
Understanding
United Order
Unity
Values
Virtue
Visions
War
Welfare services
Wickedness
Wisdom
Woman
Word of Wisdom
Work
Worry
Worship
Youth
Zion

Specific Topics for a Church Talk

Using the foregoing list of possible subjects, here are some examples of how some of these subjects might be narrowed down to a workable topic for a church talk.

Atonement: A triumph over death and hell.
Baptism: What does it mean to be born again?
Brotherhood: Insurance for the future of mankind.
Book of Mormon: Evidence that Jesus is the Christ.
Character: How the habits of today build the person of tomorrow.
Christ: How to be a disciple of the Savior.
Courage: The need for moral courage in today's world.
Education: The seminary (or institute of religion) program.
Example: "By their fruits ye shall know them."
Faith: How to develop faith in life and its purposes.
Family: How the Church and the home work together as a teaching team.
Fasting: How observance of the law of the fast gives one spiritual power.
Forgiveness: How to forgive and be forgiven.
Free agency: The making of choices.
Genealogy: Our responsibility for our ancestors.
Goals: All choices in life should be made with eternity in mind.
Holy Ghost: How to obtain the companionship of the Holy Ghost.
Home teaching: How home teachers are watchmen over the Church.
Honesty: How to be honest in one's business dealings.
Judgment: "Judge not . . . condemn not."
Leadership: Following the counsel of the Brethren.
Love: The greatest covenant, the covenant of love.
Marriage: How to prepare for temple marriage.
Morality: It is popular to be virtuous.
Obedience: Obedience to commandments must be voluntary.
Peace: Peace is rooted in righteousness.
Prophets: The role of living prophets in the world today.
Prayer: Family prayers as a cure for family maladies.
Repentance: How to correct wrongdoings.
Revelation: The power of continuous revelation.

Sacrament: The sacrament, a memorial to the Savior.

Service: The rewards of losing one's life in service to others.

Sin: The consequences of sin.

Stewardship: What is the law of stewardship?

Temple: The privilege of making covenants in the temple.

Temptation: How to avoid temptations.

Testimony: How to keep and increase one's testimony.

Thrift: Learning to balance a budget.

Truth: Truth or consequences.

Word of Wisdom: A principle with a promise.

Youth: The obligations of youth to parents and leaders.

CHAPTER 5

Finding Material

A powerful preacher, Henry Ward Beecher, once said, "Though a man be born a genius, a natural orator and a natural reasoner, these endowments give him but the outlines of himself." He went on to explain that the "filling up demands incessant, painstaking, steady work."

Having a clear purpose and the right subject are only the first steps in preparing a good talk. The real work comes in finding the right material to use. There are many basic resources available, including personal experience and contacts, printed materials, and broadcast media.

Novice speakers sometimes think that finding the right phrase or the proper illustration comes easily. However, many hours of searching, reading, and praying are part of the price a good speaker pays for motivating and inspiring material. Finding speech material need not be burdensome if one develops the habit of collecting important information regularly, and not just when he is given a specific speaking assignment.

Perhaps the most important point to remember in gathering material is that all material, regardless of source, must be consistent with what the Lord has revealed. Modern scripture specifically emphasizes the importance of teaching correct doctrine. Unsound doctrine and speculation mislead and misdirect. A speaker might judge his material by asking, Does it give me a desire to follow the Savior? Is it inspiring? Is it true?

Let's consider some resources for finding appropriate material.

Personal Experience

Your easiest and most convenient source of material for a talk is right at hand—you!

Your own background is your greatest potential resource, but if you are like most speakers, it is a source that is often overlooked. Begin with a mental inventory of what you know—your own personal knowledge and ideas—about the subject before you rush to the bookshelf. Remember, reading is not a substitute for thinking.

Recall pertinent experiences and determine meanings of words and ideas. Make your speech different simply by putting some of yourself into it. However, be prayerful and wise in using personal experiences. Some may be sacred and of such a special spiritual nature that they should not be made public, but should be shared only on special occasions under the direction of the Spirit.

Personal Contacts

Another valuable resource is people. The knowledge and experience of people around you can often provide inspiring material. In relating with others, learn to profit from two important areas: conversation and observation.

Conversation is one of the easiest ways to gain information. After you select a subject for a talk, begin discussing it with your friends, church leaders, and others with whom you come in contact. Much inspiration comes with learning to talk freely with others. Conversing about gospel topics may help you crystallize your own thoughts, be more committed to your ideas, or perhaps even change your point of view. Remember also that conversation is two-way. It is just as important to listen effectively as it is to express your own ideas.

Observation provides much worthwhile material for many speakers. The great teachers and prophets of old found much of their lesson material in life situations. The power of Jesus' teachings came from his ability to observe real-life situations and draw from them profound and vital lessons. Effective modern leaders also learn to draw analogies from everyday living. Learn to be

25

observant and then train yourself to see pertinent applications in your experiences.

Printed Materials

Printed speech material can be found in three sources:

1. *Church periodicals and magazines.*

The *Ensign* is the official voice of the Church and is written basically for adult members. Its purpose is to make available conference talks, gospel doctrine, timely messages from Church leaders, and special features to assist every individual spiritually and secularly.

The *New Era* provides teenagers with insights into contemporary issues and their relevance to the gospel. It presents church policies and answers to doctrinal questions as well as fiction, poetry, and features of special interest to youth twelve to eighteen years of age.

The *Friend* explains and illustrates the gospel in interesting ways for children under twelve.

The *Church News,* a weekly periodical, describes events of the Church throughout the world and reports conference talks, editorials, and human interest and conversion stories. Also connected with the *Church News* is the yearly *Deseret News Church Almanac,* which contains valuable information, such as the year in review, biographies of General Authorities, a historical chronology of the Church, Church membership figures, and information on missions and stakes.

Conference Reports contains the semiannual report of talks and the proceedings at general conference.

You can save much time in gathering your speech material by using the meetinghouse library, which has current church publications as well as old periodicals, such as the *Improvement Era* and the *Instructor.* The *Guide to Church Periodicals,* available in every meetinghouse library, offers a current index and cumulative index of material on specific gospel subjects. It lists articles according to subject matter, with the author, name of periodical, date of issue, and page numbers.

2. *Church books and manuals.*

Detailed information on specific topics can be obtained from books written by Church members, especially General Authorities. Avoid the tendency to take stories and ideas from Church books and use them as your own. Books should be used for reference and research, but the wording and text of your talk should be your own.

Church manuals, such as the family home evening manual, are particularly valuable for clear and simple illustrations and examples. The priesthood and auxiliary manuals offer excellent discussions on scriptures and clarification of church doctrine.

3. *Public print media.*

General non-church materials, such as books, magazines, newspapers, and reference books, may be helpful if they are in harmony with church doctrine. Often, local and national events provide illustrations to make gospel concepts more relevant to the listener. *Readers Guide to Periodical Literature* and the card catalog in your local library can help you find specific information. Quotations can be found in such books as *Bartlett's Familiar Quotations* and Edward's *Dictionary of Thoughts.*

Vital Speeches of the Day, found in the public library, is published twice monthly and contains complete texts of some of the best current speeches. It is an excellent source of quotations and information on current national issues.

Broadcast Media

Radio, television, and films may provide information and ideas for your talk. Listening to general conference broadcasts not only gives you excellent examples of speech-making, but also provides insights and instruction regarding church policies. Special church movies also provide valuable information and often inspire greater emotional and spiritual commitment. News broadcasts, documentaries, and special features may provide helpful knowledge of current events and contemporary issues.

Gathering information is only of value if you have an effective system for filing talk ideas and information. How often have you heard an impressive statement and thought, "I must remember that one"? Then two weeks later, when you have a need to quote it, you cannot remember the wording or source. Many speakers spend useless hours trying to relocate an illustration or quotation that should have been preserved in some permanent file bank.

Get in the habit of writing ideas, quotations, and other material, and then begin your own speech source file. Many speakers find it is effective to organize a file by using note cards. Loose-leaf notebooks are cumbersome and lead to the undesirable habit of writing more than one item on a page. The extent of your notes should be governed by the complexity of the subject, your prior knowledge of it, and the amount of time you have. The important thing is to write enough so that you can clearly interpret your notes later.

The card file may be used to record direct quotations, paraphrased ideas, stories, impressions, and observations. The following suggestions may be helpful in notetaking:

1. Use cards of uniform size. Keep them in a file drawer, box, or expandable envelope.

2. At the top of each file card, put a word or phrase describing the subject of the card, such as "prayer," "love," "faith."

3. At the bottom, acknowledge the author, source, page number.

4. Card example:

FAITH

By faith we come to God. If we did not believe in the Lord Jesus Christ, if we had no faith in him or in his atonement, we would not be inclined to pay any heed to his command-ments. It is because we have that faith that we are brought into harmony with his truth and have a desire in our hearts to serve him. . . . (Joseph Fielding Smith, *Doctrines of Salvation*, vol. 2, pp. 302-303.)

Remember, a speech file is like a garden—if you want to reap, you have to plant. Start planting now, keep sowing all year round, and enjoy a continual harvest of help.

In gathering material and compiling a file, keep in mind the adage "A motivating speaker is a motivated reader." A valuable source file is possible only if you have disciplined yourself to consciously seek information. Reading is a vital part of the seeking process.

Elder Hugh B. Brown has said, "Reading minds are growing minds, and when we cease to read, we cease to grow. If we do not read well, we will not think well." Get in the habit of reading and of building your own personal library, beginning with the standard works. Read something worthwhile each day during a regular time period. If you only read fifteen to twenty minutes a day, you can complete as many as twenty books a year!

As you begin a chapter or article, preview the material to get a general idea of the contents. Read the first two paragraphs, skim the following paragraphs, and then read the last two paragraphs. Ask mental questions about the subject as you preview it, such as, What are the key statements? What are some of the instructions I should write down? Underline or mark so you can return to pertinent places to transfer the idea onto a file card.

As you consciously gather material from the aforementioned sources, maintain a useful file, and improve your reading habits, you will find an abundance of information appropriate to gospel talks. In the Doctrine and Covenants, the Lord speaks regarding the gathering of worthwhile material: "And as all have not faith, seek ye diligently and teach one another words of wisdom; yea, seek ye out of the best books words of wisdom; seek learning, even by study and also by faith." (D&C 88:118.)

CHAPTER 6

Supporting Material

The old adage "A picture is worth a thousand words" is also true in church speaking. In this case, the picture is not a tangible visual aid, but a vivid, colorful mental image created in the mind's eye of the listener.

The audience may appear interested in the speaker's main points, but when he says, "Let me illustrate," they perk up to see the "picture." Just as a bridge must be supported by columns, so a speech must be supported by good examples and illustrative material.

Now that you have decided on a subject, a plan, and some basic source tools, such as magazines, books, periodicals, and speeches, the question is how to make your ideas come to life graphically for your audience.

In searching for suitable illustrative material, remember that it must help the listener understand, believe, and remember. Seven types of supporting material you might consider are:

1. Analogy or comparison
2. Parable
3. Stories
4. Poetry
5. Examples
6. Facts
7. Testimony

Let's take a closer look at each of these categories for further explanations and examples of how they can be used effectively in church speaking.

Analogy or Comparison

This method was a popular teaching aid of the Savior and is ideal for painting a concrete image of an abstract term. The technique is to liken the abstract subject to something well-known to the audience and then to expand upon the comparison. For example:

Faith is like a *seed.* It must be constantly nourished and cared for if it is to grow and bear pleasing fruit.

Gossip is like *a cancer.* It starts as a small, innocent cell, but then it multiplies, encompasses, and destroys the whole soul unless stopped in time.

Knowledge is like *money in the bank.* If we have stored knowledge in a "savings account," we can draw on it when we need assistance.

Christ knew how to associate great ideas with familiar and mundane objects. He used the word *like* freely. Notice this example in Matthew 13:44: "Again, the kingdom of heaven is like unto treasure hid in a field; the which when a man hath found, he hideth, and for joy thereof goeth and selleth all that he hath, and buyeth that field."

By using this likening method, you can greatly increase your effectiveness as a speaker.

Parables

Perhaps the most valuable way to learn about parables is to study the parables of Jesus, which are noteworthy for their simplicity and profound truth. Such parables as the Ten Virgins, the Prodigal Son, and the Talents have become classics in world and religious literature.

In the Parable of the Lost Sheep Jesus presents one facet of his great mission of saving the souls of mankind. He illustrates the joy of finding the wayward and bringing them back.

How think ye? if a man have an hundred sheep, and one of them be gone astray, doth he not leave the ninety and nine and

31

goeth into the mountains, and seeketh that which is gone astray?

And if so be that he find it, verily I say unto you, he rejoiceth more of that sheep, than of the ninety and nine which went not astray.

Even so it is not the will of your Father which is in heaven, that one of these little ones should perish. (Matthew 18:12-14.)

For a more detailed discussion of parables, you might refer to informative discussions on them in *Jesus the Christ* by James E. Talmage.

Stories

Everyone loves a story. It is often through stories that hearts are touched and lives changed. The best stories for speaking purposes should have five essential characteristics: (1) simplicity, (2) brevity, (3) message, (4) relevance to the audience, and (5) appropriateness to the occasion.

Most of us overlook the countless experiences in our lives that have relevance to ideas to be presented in a talk. The personal experience story is a favorite of audiences because it is true and can therefore be told with power and conviction.

To be an effective storyteller, you must have a great urge to share with others that which moves you deeply. Your stories must be filled with vitality, vivid description, and an impelling sense of reality. A story well-told is essentially a spiritual experience. The story needs to be well prepared, with good description, good use of dialogue, change of pace, and an interesting and pertinent conclusion. The story should be easy to follow and understand. It should also be fairly brief so it will not disturb the continuity and development of the main message of the speech. Study the following examples of good stories, and note the element of drama and the conclusions of both.

Death

Hasn't the Lord a right to call us home? Aren't we first of all His sons and daughters? I remember a father being unwilling to reconcile himself to the death of his only son. One day in the mountains he said to me that he had sought the Lord saying, "Why have you taken my boy, my son, my hope, my pride from me?" And there came to him the whisperings of the Spirit: "He was my son before he was yours. I loved him more than you will ever know how to love him, but if you are faithful I will give him back to you." And that father was reconciled. He was reconciled that God has a prior claim. When God calls us it is our business to say, "The Lord giveth and the Lord taketh away; blessed be the name of the Lord." That is all we can do, and if we will desire it, we will overcome and rise triumphant and victorious over all our sorrows. If we can only submit ourselves to that providence we will have peace in our hearts. (*Melvin J. Ballard—Crusader for Righteousness* [Bookcraft, 1966], p. 274.)

Faith

A man was standing on a cliff overlooking a deep canyon when a great gust of wind came up and blew him over the cliff. As he fell downward, he desperately grabbed hold of a branch of a hardwood tree growing from the side of the canyon. There he hung the rest of the day. There was no one around to help, so he began to pray to God, saying, "I know that thou hast the power to save me." As he hung there, long into the night, a voice said to him, "Do you believe that I created the gust of wind?" The man replied, "I believe." The voice said, "Do you believe that I caused this hardwood tree to grow from out of this granite cliff?" And the man, hanging on the tree with all his strength, said, "I believe." The voice said to him, "Do you believe that I can create a draft of wind to take you back to the top of the cliff again from where you fell?" The man, in great pain from holding onto the branch for such a long time, said, "I believe." And then the voice said to him, "Then let go of the branch."

Poetry

Poetry can be a useful way to create mental pictures because of its emphasis on the emotional and its almost musical rhythm. One of the strengths of verse is that it is often easy to remember because it appeals to the physical senses of the listener. Clinton Larson, poet in residence at Brigham Young University, states also that "all poetry has a moral, and all poetry should teach."

Study the following poem by Alfred Lord Tennyson, a stirring description of inner feelings with a strong moral lesson. It is often used at funeral services.

Crossing the Bar

Sunset and evening star,
    And one clear call for me,
And may there be no moaning of the bar,
    When I put out to sea.

But such a tide as moving seems asleep,
    Too full for sound and foam,
When that which drew from out the soundless deep
    Turns again home.

Twilight and evening bell,
    And after that the dark!
And may there be no sadness of farewell,
    When I embark;

For tho! from our bourne of time and place
    The flood may bear me far,
I hope to see my Pilot face to face
    When I have crossed the bar.

Examples

An audience enjoys hearing a speaker clarify his point by saying, "Let me give you an example." A speech without examples is usually filled with generalizations. Such a speech rarely holds the attention of an audience.

Examples may fall into two categories: (1) actual cases that can be documented and (2) hypothetical examples created for the occasion. In using examples, whether real or hypothetical, remember to tie the main point to the example, never leaving the listener to conclude the truth.

A speech outlined later in this volume, "Faith in Action," contains many good examples. Here are additional examples of faith in action.

1.   The Wright Brothers are successful because they had faith they could build and fly an airplane.

2.   Thomas A. Edison had faith that he could invent useful and valuable items.

3.   It was through faith that Brigham Young and the Mormon pioneers left their homes in the Midwest and crossed the plains to unknown lands.

4. The faith of Matthew Cowley enabled him to perform miracles among those with whom he labored in the South Pacific.

Facts

Ralph Waldo Emerson made this statement: "The public speaker, first of all, must have power of statement, must have the fact, and know how to tell it. In any public assembly, the speaker who has the facts and can and will state them will have his audience, though he stutters and screams."

The nature of the speech situation helps determine the number of facts to use. To an audience already familiar with the facts, all that is necessary is a restatement of the point.

Here is an example of using facts in a church talk pertaining to Joseph Fielding Smith, the tenth president of the Church.

"He was one of the oldest men to serve as President of the Council of the Twelve (age 74) and was a member longer than any other man in this dispensation (60 years).

"He was the oldest man to become president—age 93. He served for only two and a half years."

Another example of facts that can be used effectively are statistics. Statistics are more than numbers; they are facts that have been classified and compiled into significant figures. They can show relationships or interpret data. Figures sometimes prove a point better than any other material, but in using statistics, ask yourself, Are the statistics dependable? Are they clear? Are they interesting?

Remember also to cite the source of the information and the date published, as shown in this example:

"Some . . . adverse effects of use of alcoholic beverages might be mentioned. The economic impact of alcohol in the United States is tremendous. Billions of dollars are lost to industry each year in absenteeism, lower productivity, accidents and general inefficiency. Care of alcoholics in institutions represents a very large sum, which is paid by taxpayers. Nine million Americans—or almost ten percent of the nation's work force—are alcoholics. They and their problems affect the lives of another 40 million people, including many children." (Roy W. Doxey, *The Word of Wisdom Today* [Deseret Book, 1975], p. 43.)

Testimony

Testimonies may come from either the scriptures or quotations. A testimony is more than simply stating, "I believe." It is a statement of ideas, opinions, admonitions, and conclusions. Statements from authorities or experts attract attention and are helpful to reinforce a point. Citing the name of the source gives the quotation force and authority.

Quotations may be drawn from many sources in the vast reservoir of human expression—history, literature, biography, newspaper, speeches, and conversations. Apt statements by someone else may lend weight to your own views. Courts of law provide a constant reminder of the value of testimony in supporting ideas. When selecting and using a testimony, ask, Is the person cited known and respected? Is he a good source?

Another excellent source of testimonies is the scriptures. Every church talk should include scriptures, for here are found the testimony of the Lord to man and testimonies and admonitions of great prophets.

In using testimonies, avoid reading long quotations or scriptural passages, and avoid saying "quote" and "unquote." Study the following examples of introducing testimonies.

1.   Let me read to you the testimony that Peter bore: "For he received from God the Father honour and glory, when there came such a voice to him from the excellent glory. This is my beloved Son, in whom I am well pleased. And this voice which came from heaven we heard, when we were with him in the holy mount." These words are found in 2 Peter, chapter 16, verses 17 and 18.

2.   Ammon taught a great lesson not only to his brother, Aaron, but also to all of us today, in Alma, chapter 26, verses 11 and 12: "I do not boast in my own strength, nor in my own wisdom; but behold, my joy is full, yea, my heart is brim with joy, and I will rejoice in my God. Yea, I know that I am nothing; as to my strength I am weak; therefore I will not boast of my God, for in his strength I can do all things; yea, behold many mighty miracles we have wrought in this land, for which we will praise his name forever."

3.   In a revelation to the Prophet Joseph Smith just prior to the organization of the Church, the Lord said: "Ask the Father in my name, in faith believing that you shall receive, and you shall

36

have the Holy Ghost, which manifesteth all things which are expedient unto the children of men." This scriptures is in Doctrine and Covenants, section 18, verses 10 to 12.

Acknowledging the author of a quotation can be done in several ways:

1. *Preceding the reference.* George Albert Smith has said, "We live in a day when there are many temptations to evil, and each one who submits himself to any one of them loses a blessing." Or: According to George Albert Smith, "We live in a day . . ."

2. *In the middle of the reference.* "We live in a day when there are many temptations to evil," said George Albert Smith, "and each one . . ."

3. *Following the reference.* "We live in a day . . ." These are the inspired words of George Albert Smith.

You need not use all of these types of supporting material in one talk, but you should use a variety and combination appropriate to the situation. A sacrament meeting talk might easily include the use of examples, stories, poetry, and testimonials, while a fireside talk might use analogies, facts, and parables. The important point is that the listeners need a visual point of reference. They will remember the message of the speech more easily if they can picture it in their minds, through the proper use of illustrations.

CHAPTER 7

The
Introduction

In the newspaper business, it is important to be able to write a good headline and a catchy lead. The headline capsulizes the story, and the lead, or first paragraph, entices the reader to continue reading the story.

So it is with speaking. Essential to a good talk is a good beginning. It is in the first few sentences that the audience mentally judges the speaker and decides if they want to tune in or tune out.

A theologian once said, "There are three things to aim at in public speaking: first, to get into your subject; then, to get your subject into yourself; and lastly, to get your subject into your hearers."

It is interesting how many speakers fail to get into their subject. They spend valuable time rambling from one thought to the next, all for the intended purpose of "warming up to the audience."

How familiar to Church audiences is the following beginning:

My dear brothers and sisters, as I look out over the congregation, I see many more capable than I and I wonder why the bishop asked me to speak. I sat down and figured it out that it has been two years since I have spoken in sacrament meeting. The bishop asked me to talk to you tonight about faith. I sort of thought of a cute saying, "Faith without works is like an automobile without gas." Oh, that reminds me that our missionary son in Germany is doing just fine. And I want to tell all of you that you will be better members if you follow the advice I have compiled here in these notes. Oh, I heard the other day that some people use their religion like a bus. They ride on it only when it is going their way. I don't want to forget to tell you this one. My daughter helped me with this one. "Instead of being Latter-day Saints, why not be every-day Saints?" I like that. Well, I guess I had better say something about faith. The bishop asked me to talk for fifteen minutes. Gosh, I have talked for 8 minutes already. Gee, time does fly. . . .

Yes, time flies and so does the restless audience when the meeting is over!

The following are "don't" beginnings for church speakers: "I am scared to death to speak." "I apologize, but I am just not a public speaker—I don't know why the bishop called on me." "I was just asked last Thursday to speak, so forgive me if I am not too well prepared." "I was asked to speak on the subject of 'Why I believe faith is important.' " "The bishop asked if I would talk to you for about twenty minutes on 'the importance of honoring parents.' "

The how, when, and where you were asked to speak and how difficult it is for you to stand before an audience should not be confessed. Get your listeners in tune for your motivating message by using a positive approach. The purpose of the opening statement is to introduce the theme of your talk, and the first step in this direction must certainly be to win the attention of the audience for your message.

Some speakers try to use humor to gain attention. This can be used *if* the humor is relevant to the theme of the talk, but all irrelevant humor should be avoided.

The introduction should answer this question: Why should you, the audience, listen to me? In order to answer this question, prepare your beginning remarks so that they establish an interrelationship between you and your audience. Strive to be brief, friendly, and sincere. Avoid flattery, apologies, triteness, self-importance, and, as mentioned, irrelevant humor.

Since your introductory statement must rightly adjust the theme, speakers, audience, and the occasion to each other, it must be fully and carefully prepared.

An audience is mixed company, with members who have come in different states of mind. Some are tired, some are distracted, and some may not be keen to hear what you have to say. It is therefore most important to examine ways of planning interest at the beginning.

Here is a partial list of the types of introductions that may be used in the speaking situation.

1. Startling statement
2. Challenging question
3. Human interest story
4. Statement of a problem
5. Scripture, parable, quotation, or poem
6. Reference to a current event
7. Reference to a special occasion or season

Sample Speech for Study

In considering the ingredients of good introduction, let's examine our sample speech, "Faith in Action" (see Chapter 14):

I was a teenager, active in church, and with a firm testimony of Joseph Smith.

One spring afternoon, I walked to the public library to begin research for a seminary talk on Porter Rockwell. I found what I was seeking—a documented book on that subject. I eagerly poured over the pages until the shock of what I was reading stopped me cold.

Here was a book that declared that Joseph Smith was a drunkard and Porter Rockwell was a murderer! To this day, I can relive the sickening feeling that came over me. I knew the information must be false because of the teachings of my parents and church leaders. Yet, as a teenage boy with no previous exposure to anti-Mormon literature, I found myself doubting my own testimony. For that moment, my faith was being tested.

Note the elements of a good introduction. The speech gets right into the subject matter with a story approach. The use of first person makes the story even more interesting. The character, a teenage boy, draws young listeners into the story. There is an element of drama as the boy questions his basic life-style and beliefs. The audience is ready to listen to the outcome, and the speaker can now escort the audience into the essence of the talk.

So you see that the beginning of a sermon is of supreme importance—even more important than the conclusion. You must gain attention at once, or you may not gain it at all. If those in the audience have not been encouraged to listen at the beginning, it is unlikely that they will be doing so ten or twenty minutes later.

Preparing and delivering a good introduction is much like fishing. A lake fisherman knows that a common practice is "chumming," that is, throwing pieces of cheese or other bait in the water to attract the attention of the fish. The cheese lures them around the boat, so that when the hook and line hit the water, the fish are there, ready to grab.

In speaking, the introduction is the "chum" to warm up the audience and prepare them for the important message you are to deliver. If the listener is adequately prepared and lured, he will fix his attention on the "chummer," or speaker, waiting and hungering for the body of the talk and every morsel of eternal truth.

CHAPTER 8

Organizing Your Talk

"A place for everything, everything in its place." These oft-quoted words of Benjamin Franklin are reiterated by many persons, to cover many situations. Yet, how many public speakers take the advice to heart?

The philosopher Southey wrote, "Order is the sanity of the mind, the health of the body, the peace of the city, the security of the state." And, one might add, "Order is the power of a speaker and the delight of an audience." Organization and order in preparing and presenting a speech bring inward calm, confidence, command over thoughts, and a power to convince.

Stage fright and nervousness often come simply from lack of organization and order in the speaker's thoughts. Harry Emerson Fosdick once said, "I would never think of speaking without, in some way, ordering my thought."

So, after you have decided what you are going to talk about and why you are going to talk about it, you must consider how you are going to proceed. The key is simple: make a plan.

A person who drives from Los Angeles to New York City needs a highway map to follow. A person who builds a house needs a blueprint. A person who plays a concerto needs the music to follow. Even so, a person who gives a speech needs to follow a written, organized plan in order to achieve his purpose. The speech that motivates, persuades, inspires, and uplifts must center around a plan of order and organization. The speech plan may be a simple outline on a note card or a complete, word-for-word manuscript, but it must be there.

Before considering some different approaches to organizing the talk, let's consider some basic steps in preparing a speech plan.

First, write down your thoughts as they come. The logical sequence is not important at this point. Ideas for the conclusion of your talk may come initially before the introduction or body. Ideas can be sorted out and arranged later. Keep a notepad and pencil handy so you can write down thoughts when they come. How disappointed is the speaker who says, "Last night in bed, I had my entire talk planned and prepared, but this morning I can't remember a thing!"

Make a talk folder or envelope. As you read, hear, think, or observe relating to your speech topic, gather the material into a folder. As scriptures, examples, stories, and illustrations come to mind, jot them down and put them in the folder. You will soon find, as you begin to write and organize, that you have ample material to begin organizing your speech.

Next, after you have gathered ideas, arrange them in outline form. Outline the body of the talk first. Then you can see more clearly the direction you are going and identify more readily material that may need to be strengthened or deleted. You can also see what material you want to set aside for the beginning and conclusion.

Divide your central thought into several main points and illustrate each point. As a general rule, don't develop more than three or four major points. Unless you are an experienced speaker, you may lose the interest of your audience if you give them too many major points.

In your outline, use symbols and indentions to indicate relationships of ideas. For example:

I. Roman numerals are used for the main ideas.
    A.   Capital letters are used for the first subheadings.
       1. Arabic numerals mark the next subordinate ideas.
          a. Small letters are used for supportive ideas.

43

(1) If necessary, arabic numbers in
    parentheses are used next.

After you have outlined your basic material so the direction
and purposes of your talk are more clear to you, decide on a
specific approach or arrangement of your ideas. The examples that
follow are only for the body of the talk; it must also have a beginning and a conclusion.

Chronological Arrangement

Some subjects and topics are best organized in the order in
which they happened. This is called chronological arrangement.
Start with the point that came first in time, and follow in order
with the second and third. (A time arrangement can also be used in
reverse.) This type of arrangement is helpful in topics concerning
histories, missionary reports, biographies, and eulogies. Study the
following groupings, which illustrate time order:

Great Prophets
  I. Moses
 II. Joseph Smith
III. Spencer W. Kimball

Biography (any person)
  I. Early years
 II. Middle age
III. Old age

Church History
  I. Saints leaving Nauvoo
 II. Travel to Salt Lake Valley
III. Arrival in Salt Lake Valley

Problem-Solution Arrangement

Sometimes you can best organize a speech by dividing it into
two major parts: (1) stating the problem and (2) suggesting a solution. Many topics may be organized this way, such as the following:

1. Paying a full tithe
2. Keeping the Word of Wisdom
3. Marrying in the temple
4. Following our prophet
5. Repentance

A problem-solution talk could be outlined in this manner:
I. Define the problem.
II. Explain what standard is expected
III. Suggest workable solutions
Here is a sample outline illustrating this approach:
Topic: Following Our Prophet
I.   Many church members are not following our prophet in the following situations:
   A.   Holding family home evening
   B.   Holding regular family prayer
   C.   Participating in home beautification
   D.   Obtaining a food and fuel supply
   E.   Honoring their mate
II.   The Lord expects us to follow the prophet
   A.   Scriptures defining what a prophet is
   B.   Importance of listening to the prophet
   C.   Quotations of our prophet
III.   We must meet the problem in this way:
   A.   Develop a greater testimony of the prophet
   B.   Listen to the prophet
   C.   Study his word
   D.   Repent
   E.   Commit ourselves to following diligently

Text Arrangement

It is not uncommon to hear a speaker declare, "I shall take as a text" and then proceed to quote a scripture. This method builds a speech around a particular scripture or literary excerpt. The text then may be divided into parts, each becoming a major point in the speech. After the theme has been stated in your own words, it should be analyzed and discussed in the light of its context. Here is a sample text that could be developed in this way as the body of the talk:

Topic: The Resurrection of Jesus Christ
Text: For I delivered unto you first of all that which I also received, how that Christ died for our sins according to the scriptures; And that he was buried, and that he rose again the third day according to scriptures. (1 Corinthians 15:3-4.)

I. The nature and proof of the resurrection of Jesus Christ
II. The necessity for the resurrection of Jesus Christ
III. The results of Jesus Christ's resurrection

Topical Arrangement

This is the most common and popular method to organize the body of a speech. It is often referred to as the psychological order because the material is arranged according to listener interest.

This type of organization is used most often by those who preside, such as General Authorities, mission presidents, Regional Representatives, stake presidents, bishops, and other stake and ward leaders. It allows the speaker to cover a wide range of different subjects, rather than one, or to speak on one subject but discuss many topics within that subject. One example of the topical plan is used when a presiding authority focuses attention on matters of timely and general interest, to warn of impending danger, and to arouse interest in the duties of the hour.

An excellent example of using the topical plan is the speech by President Spencer W. Kimball given at general conference in 1974.

Title: "God Will Not Be Mocked"
I. In our personal lives
II. In the home
III. In the community
IV. In the Church

Remember, nothing of importance and lasting value is done without a plan. In planning your speech, accumulate material and ideas in a thought folder. Organize your material by outlining the body of the talk. Decide on the best approach—chronological, problem-solution, text, or topical. Organize the outline to fit the best approach. Add a beginning and a conclusion. And review the finished product carefully, cutting out any material that does not directly apply to your subject.

Now you have a plan for effective speaking—"a place for everything, and everything in its place." By following closely your road map as you prepare and polish your speech, you will be well on the way to a happy, successful, and gratifying journey.

46

CHAPTER 9

Your Conclusion

Ringing in the listener's ear as the speaker takes his seat are those last words of challenge and conclusion.

As important as the introduction and body of the talk are, we must not underestimate the force of the conclusion, for a speaker can lose what he has gained in the last few minutes if he has not carefully preplanned his conclusion. No matter how powerful the sermon, a weak ending can leave the audience feeling indifferent instead of uplifted and motivated.

The conclusion is that part of a speech in which a review is made and the truth is applied to the lives of the listeners. It does not merely end the speech, but it also restates the purpose and theme and engraves them in the minds and consciences of the listeners.

It might be wise to write down the last several sentences of the speech and then memorize them. Then you will know where and how to finish, without groping for a good place to stop.

In preparing a conclusion, avoid negative and apologetic remarks, humor, nervous mannerisms, and adding new concepts and ideas.

Church sermons should always be closed with the words, "In the name of Jesus Christ. Amen." This is not a substitute for a conclusion, but an acknowledgment of our source of wisdom.

Your speech needs a transition between your closing statement and that final closure. For example, a talk on tithes and offerings might be concluded with "That we might all be more diligent in paying our tithes and offerings is my prayer, in the name of Jesus Christ. Amen."

Do not leave your audience dangling without a conclusion before that final phrase. Your conclusion may have a combination of these points:

1. Issuing a challenge or appeal
2. Summarizing
3. Using a quotation or scripture
4. Using an illustration
5. Poetry
6. Testimony

Challenge or Appeal

Many church speakers make an appeal to the audience to live a certain ideal by applying to their daily lives the precepts and ideals expounded. They openly appeal for belief or action, or remind their listeners of their responsibilities in furthering the desired end. Such a challenge should be vivid and should include a suggestion of the principal ideas presented in the speech.

The conclusion of the sample speech "Faith in Action" makes use of the "appeal" closure:

As we consider the level of our faith, let us determine to seek greater knowledge, keep the commandments, and change passive belief into active faith. As our faith develops, we will enjoy a greater understanding of the purposes of life, a greater ability to resist temptation and live the commandments, and a greater peace of mind in days of trial.

Let us remember that without faith, nothing of worth can be accomplished. With faith, all things are possible. Faith is the first principle of the gospel because it is faith that gives us the motivation and power to do the things we must in order to be saved.

May we have the faith to create and contribute. May we increase our faith in the gospel of Jesus Christ, faith in church leaders, faith in our country, and most of all, faith in ourselves, I pray, in the name of Jesus Christ. Amen.

48

Summary

In a summary conclusion, review the main point or points of your talk and emphasize their bearing on the theme. The summary has the further advantage of helping the audience remember the important points of the talk and how they are to be applied.

Quotation or Scripture

A quotation or scripture may be used to end your speech if it bears directly on the central idea of the speech. Often this method can summarize the whole theme that one is discussing. Scriptures or quotations used at the end of a speech should be short, memorable, and pertinent.

Illustration and Poetry

Use this type of conclusion to create for the listener a picture or thought in his mind that makes it easier to remember the theme.

Testimony

Often the power of one's own personal testimony is an effective conclusion. In bearing your testimony, bear only that portion of testimony that is pertinent to the theme. For instance, in a talk on prayer, you might effectively end your talk with a personal experience that shows the power of prayer and then conclude, "I can testify to the power of prayer in our lives, for the Lord has answered my own prayers, and this I testify in the name of Jesus Christ. Amen."

Excellent examples of various kinds of conclusions may be found in general conference talks reported in the *Ensign* or in *Conference Reports.*

The effective conclusion should make use of all your abilities to inspire and communicate clearly. Do not rush the conclusion, as if you are eager to get the speech over, but plan your talk so you have sufficient time to conclude with ease, with confidence, and with conviction. Be specific, be brief, and above all be sincere. Your conclusion should always suggest a better way of living and an appeal for acceptance of a belief or principle.

SUMMARY OUTLINE FOR PREPARING A TALK

Main Idea or Point (write down, in the fewest possible words, the point you wish to make): _____

_____

Topic: _____

Introduction (briefly note a story, example, scripture, quotation, or fact to introduce your topic): _____

_____

Body (for each point to be developed, list scriptures, quotations, stories, examples, facts, illustrations)

Point 1: _____

Stories, scriptures, etc.: _____

_____

_____

_____

Point 2: _____

Stories, scriptures, etc.: _____

_____

_____

_____

Point 3: _____

_____

_____

Conclusion, (summary, testimony, final words—"In the name of Jesus Christ. Amen"): _____

_____

_____

50

CHAPTER 10

The
Power of Words

"A man cannot speak but he judges and reveals himself. With his will, or against his will, he draws his portrait to the eye of others by every word."

Ralph Waldo Emerson was well aware of the power of words as they related to his own self-image and as they influenced his listeners for good or bad. In contemporary life we see many "portraits" drawn as we listen to church speakers and are greatly influenced by their *words*.

The Lord has emphasized the importance of verbal communication as a means of teaching his children and drawing them back to him. Through words, people may decide to pray or to turn from sin. Words from the pulpit may make people work, laugh, think, aspire, and hope. Through effective words, people build faith in themselves and in mankind.

As part of a vast army of church speakers, we must realize the far-reaching effects of the speaker's word. To help us develop greater word power, we should read the scriptures and sermons of our church leaders and strive to improve our own pulpit performance.

Job complained about the "vain words" of his so-called comforters, and then exclaimed, "How forcible are right words!" (Job 6:25.) The wise preacher is described as seeking out "acceptable words" by which to convey his message, "even words of truth."

(Ecclesiastes 12:10.) Paul urged those who preached the word of God to do so by means of words that were "easy to be understood." (1 Corinthians 14:9.) The language used in speaking must be simple. The divine dictum is, ". . . except ye utter by the tongue words easy to be understood, how shall it be known what is spoken? For ye shall speak into the air."

Let's consider some ideas to help improve our word usage—diction, grammar, semantics, and pronunciation.

First, remember the power of simplicity. Simple phrases are often those that are immortal:

"Four score and seven years ago . . ."

"The Lord is my shepherd; I shall not want."

"To be, or not to be: that is the question."

The greatest of all speeches, the Sermon on the Mount, is amazingly simple and direct:

"Blessed are the poor in spirit: for theirs is the kingdom of heaven.

"Blessed are they that mourn: for they shall be comforted.

"Blessed are the meek; for they shall inherit the earth." (Matthew 5:3-5.)

A rule of thumb for speakers is: Don't use long words when short ones will do. When Jesus spoke, "the common people heard him gladly." (Mark 12:37.) Though he could be so profound as to reduce the most learned of his critics to confused silence, his language was so simple that no one was left in doubt. (See Matthew 22:26.)

Second, be specific. For example, in the parable of the Good Samaritan, don't call him a man—call him a Samaritan. Don't say "along a highway" if you can say "Along a road from Jerusalem to Jericho." Use picture words instead of abstracts. Dress up your points with similes and metaphors.

Third, always speak kindly, avoiding any words and statements that might give offense. Someone once said, "Before speaking, ask yourself: Is it true? Is it kind? Is it necessary?" Many a thoughtless speaker has learned the truth of the adage, "Kind words can never die and the other kind live forever."

Choose your words with these questions in mind: (1) Is my thought clear? Does it clearly express my intention in a positive way? (2) Does it promote goodwill? Is it free from class, sectional, racial, or national bitterness? (3) Is it spiritual? Does it clarify or make a principle of the gospel more appealing?

Grammar

As you use simple, specific, and thoughtful words, you will begin to feel the positive power of the words you communicate. As you study the use of words, study also some of the practical problems connected with word usage. Many a speaker with a valuable message has failed to reach his audience because of one simple fault—poor grammar.

Incorrect grammar can ruin the best talk by distracting the listeners from the spirit and intent of the talk. Some common grammatical errors in public speaking are these:

Grammatical Error	Incorrect	Correct
Use of double negatives	He *hadn't hardly* got there.	He *hardly* got there.
	There *wasn't no* one inside.	There *was no* one inside.
Misuse of adverb for adjective form	I feel *badly.*	I feel *bad.*
	He felt *poorly* this morning.	He felt *poor* this morning.
Extra and useless prepositions	Where did he go *to?*	Where did he go?
	Where is the paper *at?*	Where is the paper?
Improper case of pronouns	They rode with Mary and *I.*	They rode with Mary and *me.*
	Mary and *me* are going to ride.	Mary and *I* are going to ride.
	Mary is going to ride with Dick and *I.*	Mary is going to ride with Dick and *me.*
Plural subject with singular verb	We *was* there.	We *were* there.
	John and Sandy *was* coming.	John and Sandy *were* coming.

Grammatical Error	Incorrect	Correct
	There *goes* two ducks.	There *go* two ducks.
Split infinitives	He decided *to not do* the work.	He decided *not to do* the work.
	Tom said that I was *to never talk* to him again.	Tom said that I was *never to talk* to him again.

Tense is very important in using correct grammar. Some of the common errors are made in the use of the verbs *saw* and *seen*, *did* and *done*. How many times have you heard a speaker say, "I seen it myself" or "They've did it many times," rather than "I *saw* it myself" and "They've *done* it many times."

Forms of the verbs *lay* and *lie* are especially troublesome. *Lay* means "to place something" and is always followed by an object. *Lie* means "to rest" and has no object. Look at these verb forms:

Present Tense	Past	Past Perfect	Participle
lie	lay	had lain	lying
lay	laid	had laid	laying

Test yourself on these tenses. Which would you use?
1. Will you (lie, lay) down?
2. I (lay, laid) down for an hour.
3. She had (laid, lain) in bed all day.
4. Please (lay, lie) the book on the table.°

As the chart indicates, subject-verb agreement is an important area also. Two commonly heard mistakes from the pulpit are "We feel it in our heart" and "They will remember it all their life." The subject must agree in number with the verb, and vice versa. The correct form is: "We feel it in our *hearts*," and "They will remember it all their *lives*."

A problem area that deserves special attention is the proper use of pronouns. Two pronouns that often give trouble are the ques-

° The correct answers are (1) lie, (2) lay, (3) lain, and (4) lay.

tion forms of who and whom. *Who* should be used as the subject of the verb, and *whom* should be the object of the verb. Notice these examples: Who was there? Whom did you see?

While we do not want to present a textbook chapter on grammar, it is important to review a few errors that are becoming widespread in church speaking. As we correct our grammar, we increase our abilities as public speakers.

Semantics

Let's move into another area of word usage, semantics, which is the study of (1) the conditions under which words may be used correctly and (2) the human behavior caused by words.

Speakers who are not specific but are vague in their descriptions are usually guilty of using poor semantics, because the message has not been clearly understood.

If you hear the word *dispensation,* you need to know specifically what dispensation, to give you a point of reference and clarify your thinking. Two areas tend toward misunderstandings—names and abstractions.

In using the names, if you refer to "President Smith," you risk the audience's settling on a number of mental references—Joseph Smith, George Albert Smith, Joseph F. Smith, or Joseph Fielding Smith. Specify exactly *whom* and *what* you mean.

In speaking of abstract ideas, illustrate and define. Words such as happiness, faith, love, truth, sin, morality, good, evil, and pornography might have many different connotations and do not necessarily mean the same thing to all persons.

Semantically speaking, what a word means to you is the sum total of the experiences you have had. The word *snow* might mean one thing to a Californian and something entirely different to an Eskimo.

Likewise, the word *Mormon* has a different meaning to a non-member than to a member. *Freedom* does not mean the same thing to everyone. To some people, *honesty* means absolute honor; to others, it is a mere technicality. The word *immorality* can mean anything from poor business ethics to illicit sex relations.

Never assume that the listener views things the same way you do. Always define, explain, and clearly illustrate.

Trite Expressions

Along with semantics, consider the use of trite expressions and slang, for these two problem areas can also diminish your effectiveness as a speaker.

A trite expression is one that has been used so often it is stale and ineffective. Here are some common trite expressions to avoid:

1. I'm grateful for this opportunity to be with you tonight.
2. As I look out over the congregation, I see many more capable than I. I wonder why I was asked to speak.
3. I feel humble in speaking tonight.
4. Pardon me for reading my talk. I have difficulty in remembering what I want to say.
5. I hope you won't mind if I quote quite a bit. Others can explain things much better than I possibly could.
6. I hope you will bear with me.
7. It's been a long time since I have spoken in church.
8. I don't want to take too much of your time.

Slang expressions should also be avoided. As a speaker, your purpose is to elevate and uplift. Slang expressions tend to pull the listener back down to earth. Visualize the real-life situation of the adult adviser who stood before her thirteen-year-old girls and said, "You guys have just got to act more ladylike!"

Pronunciation

Finally, an important consideration is proper pronunciation of words. Poor pronunciation distracts listeners and gives a bad impression, which no one can afford. How effective was the woman who stood to speak about "proper eti-quit," or the man who exclaimed, "if there's anything I can't stand, it is bad pronounciation!"

To improve your pronunciation, listen closely to good radio and television announcers, educated persons you know, and church leaders at general conference.

Check yourself for these common errors:

Incorrect	Correct
goin' or gonna	going
runnen	running

riden	riding
are	our (or hour)
git	get
jist	just
probly	probably
comfortbly	comfortably
patriartichal	patriarchal
Melchezdik	Melchizedek

Ask friends and family to help you be aware of mistakes in daily speaking. Check the dictionary for correct pronunciations before you speak. For anyone who speaks or writes, a dictionary is indispensable. Since language is always changing, be sure to keep a current dictionary within easy reach. Make word books part of your personal library. If you find you are wearing out a word with constant repetition, replace it with a better one. Among the best-known synonym books are *Roget's Thesaurus of the English Language in Dictionary Form, Funk and Wagnall's Standard Handbook of Synonyms, Antonyms, and Prepositions,* and *Webster's Dictionary of Synonyms.*

Use of Divine Titles

We sometimes hear a talk or sermon in which the full title of Christ, "The Lord Jesus Christ," is repeated at every reference to him. Be sensitive to using a variety of expressions when referring to Deity. Not only does this practice place greater emphasis on the divine personage, but in itself it can be a great teaching device. The Lord says:

Wherefore, let all men beware how they take my name in their lips—

Remember that which cometh from above is sacred, and must be spoken with care, and by constraint of the Spirit; and in this there is no condemnation, and ye receive the Spirit through prayer; wherefore, without this there remaineth condemnation. (D&C 63:61, 64.)

Note the many titles for the Holy Ghost: Holy Spirit of Promise, Spirit of Truth, the Comforter, the Testator, the Holy Spirit, the Sanctifier.

57

The Father could be referred to as Father in heaven, Heavenly Father, God, the Father, the Eternal Father, Holy Father, the Almighty.

How much better to refer to the Lord Jesus Christ as Christ, the Son of Man, the Lord, the Savior, our Lord and Master, the Master, the Son of God, the Lamb of God, Jehovah, Jesus of Nazareth, King of kings, the Messiah, Son of the Father.

A wise man once said, "Words may be either servants or masters. If the former they may safely guide us in ways of truth. If the latter, they may lead us into swamps of thought where we have no footing."

As speakers, let us build our thoughts on solid foundations by using words as tools for conveying our important messages.

58

CHAPTER 11

Using Humor Effectively

Golden K. Driggs, a former mission president, was speaking of his missionary experiences in Baltimore, Maryland:

I recall the day Charles Lindbergh flew to Paris. The newspapers around the world headlined, "Lindbergh flies the Atlantic ALONE." On the day he landed in Paris (May 21, 1927), my missionary companion and I landed in jail in Baltimore, Maryland. We had held a street meeting without a permit so we were placed in jail. A trial was held and we were released after paying a small fine. It was then that we heard the newsboys shouting that Lindbergh had landed in Paris. So we have boasted ever since that the day Lindbergh landed in Paris, we landed in jail!

After I was released from my missionary activity, I attended a meeting where the stake president was talking about Lindbergh's goodwill flight and the great diplomatic good he had accomplished. He said, "Lindbergh was not alone as he flew from New York to Paris. The Lord was with him." I happened to be a speaker at this same meeting, so as I stood I said, "Now I know where the Lord was the day we were thrown in jail for preaching on the street corner. He was with Lindbergh, and not with us."

This story is typical of hundreds of fun-filled Latter-day Saint situations that bring smiles to the countenance and warmth to the heart. From the early days of the Church, humor and laughter have played important roles in the lives of Latter-day Saints. Often, humor has been the ballast to get people through intense and trying times.

Abraham Lincoln once said, "With the fearful strain that is on me night and day, if I did not laugh I should die."

Humor does have a place in life, and it even has a place in church speaking. Important to our goal of becoming better church speakers is learning the proper touch in our speaking. However, few members realize there is an art to learning that proper touch.

Humor used appropriately and in good taste can weld and unify the audience, break down the stern guards of the mind, and open the way for the passage of truth and appeal. A touch of humor may give an audience a pause, a rest, a time to take a deep breath and then come back with renewed energy to listen to another portion of the message.

One speaker, after using a humorous illustration in his speech, remarked, "I enjoy hearing them laugh, for when they do, their mouths are open; and while they are open, I can pop the truth down."

Effective speakers apply humorous illustrations at appropriate times in a way their audience never forgets. However, there are limits to the use of humor in church. Using true humor, not just "being funny," may be one of the strongest weapons of persuasion because it brings genuine whole-souled emotions out of reserve. Real humor is not the same as fun or hilarity. A funny man can seldom persuade one to do anything more serious than laugh. We are told by the Lord to "cease from light-mindedness." (D&C 88:121.)

Humor that draws attention to itself and exists only for its own sake should be avoided. Never tell a humorous story unless it has a purpose.

Sarcasm has no place at the pulpit, and humor that belittles sin or tones down eternal truths is entirely out of place. Remember that you do not occupy the pulpit to entertain, but to teach the word of God. There is a subtle temptation in church speaking to "play to the gallery," but this must be conscientiously avoided.

Also, while humorous remarks can serve the speaker in many ways at the beginning or middle of a speech, they are never justified at the conclusion; there the speaker must neither divert nor amuse.

The late Marvin O. Ashton, of the Presiding Bishopric, was a good example of an individual who could use humor well. At a general conference in April 1945, he told the following story.

I am not like the gentleman who had a wife like the wife that Brother Thomas E. McKay spoke about in conference. He didn't want her nagging at him. He wanted her away from the battle so he could fight in peace. He had a wife who thought she was better than he. Before she died, she had put on her tombstone, "Follow me." You see, she wanted him to land in the celestial realms she was dead sure of. He wasn't quite satisfied with the epitaph as it was, so he finished it. It then read, "To follow thee I'm not content, until I know which way you went."

Here are some basic rules regarding the use of humor in giving a talk:

1. Do prepare your story. Be sure it is pertinent to the subject.
2. Do keep it simple and follow a logical sequence.
3. Do personalize it as much as possible.
4. Do make it sound spontaneous, not forced.
5. Do use humor sparingly.
6. Do not announce that a humorous story is coming up.
7. Do not tell a story in which you are the "hero."
8. Do not laugh at your own jokes.
9. Do not tell a story that will offend anyone.

President David O. McKay was noted for his spontaneous sense of humor. Norman Vincent Peale tells this story:

I recall a heart-stopping moment when as the aged President McKay mounted the platform to address a group, he tripped on the stairs. There was a gasp from the people. But he stood up and faced the audience with that irrepressible smile. "It's awful to grow old," he said ruefully, *"but I prefer it to the alternative."* (Improvement Era, *February 1970, p. 24.*)

Remember, lively, spontaneous humor is closely allied to enthusiasm. Both require a keen and alert mind. Much of Christ's strength as the Master Teacher and speaker came in spontaneity used wisely. His sermons grew out of immediate happenings. Such is our challenge also—our humor should follow this effective style of speaking.

Carl W. Buehner of the Presiding Bishopric used humor well in his sermons, as the following story illustrates.

I would like to relate a story that I have told a number of times, which some of you have heard before, but it has a point to it worth consideration.

It is about the golfer who went out on the golf course and placed his ball on a tee. He raised his club and drove the ball way down the fairway, and when he finally found it, it was in the center of a large anthill. He stepped up close to it, took another club out of his bag, and swung at the ball. He missed it and tore out a third of the anthill. He stepped up a little closer. He raised his club and swung a second time. He missed the ball again and mutilated the anthill on the other side. By that time the remaining ants in the anthill became very much alarmed at what was happening to their homes, their relatives, their friends, and they called together their leaders very hurriedly for a solution. A moment later the leaders made this report: "If you want to be saved, you had better get on the ball."

Think it over, brethren and sisters. I think that would fit our lives in many ways. Think it over, and then conform your lives with the time that has been allotted to you. Stay on the straight and narrow pathway that leads us back again into the presence of our Heavenly Father to enjoy with him the great blessings of the righteous and the faithful. (Improvement Era, June 1955, p. 415.)

CHAPTER 12

The Importance of Time

An important consideration in preparing and delivering a talk is the amount of time you have been allotted. This is one area that is often abused by Church speakers—but should be foremost in the speaker's mind.

Benjamin Franklin once said, "Dost thou love life? Then do not squander time, for that is the stuff life is made of."

When a speaker faces an audience of 240 people and speaks for 15 minutes, he is working with some 600 hours of vital teaching time. Thus, there are two times you need to be concerned with—preparation time and presentation time. If you do not use the hours and days prior to your talk to organize, pray, and prepare, you will not be able to use your speaking time most effectively.

Perhaps one of the great errors church speakers make is in not stopping on time. It is essential that you know exactly how long you are to speak and that you adhere to the time limitations.

On one occasion a speaker, sitting quietly before the meeting began, turned to the bishop and whispered, "How long do you want me to talk?"

The bishop replied, "You can talk all night if you want to, but the congregation usually leaves about 5:30."

You may spend weeks preparing your talk and perfecting your delivery, but if you speak too long, you will lose your audience and defeat your hours of preparation.

In a sense, speaking too long is an act of selfishness. It should be the speaker's duty to keep the faith of the audience and those in charge by adhering to the time schedule. Someone asked the usher in the foyer of a chapel if the man who was scheduled to speak had finished. "Oh, yes," he replied, "he finished ten minutes ago, but he hasn't stopped yet." Happy is the man who knows when he has finished and stops!

When a meeting is to be shared by two or more speakers, it is an inexcusable act of discourtesy for one to monopolize the time, leaving the other with only a small portion of the time rightfully belonging to him. Do not be guilty of platform robbery, which is, in itself, a form of dishonesty.

Popular is the speaker who has developed the art of making his finishing point and stopping point coincide. A formula for a good speech is to get a good beginning and a better ending—and keep them as close together as possible.

Many people in the average congregation are unaccustomed to extended periods of concentration, and even if the speech is interesting, the strain produces fatigue. This condition may be reached by some after about twenty minutes, and for them, even an extra five minutes may lessen the effectiveness of a good sermon or speech. One bishop commented that "few people are converted after a twenty-five-minute talk."

Why do people object to long sermons? One reason is because of boredom. If the speech runs too long they have much greater opportunity to find fault than if it lasts just long enough. It should be long enough to present the message adequately and short enough to be interesting. Every church speaker would do well to keep in mind the following prayer when he speaks: "Lord, fill my mouth with proper stuff, and nudge me when I've said enough."

So as you put the finishing touches on your speech, be sensitive to the time. Then your audience will appreciate you, and you will feel more satisfied and eager to accept another call to speak.

An Effective Delivery

An old country preacher was telling the story of David and Goliath. He related how David whirled the sling around his head and sent the stone flying at Goliath's forehead. Reaching the climax of his sermon, his voice arose high with excitement. "You see, folks, the point is this. It wasn't just that little rock that kilt that big bloke—it was the way that blankety-blank kid throwed it!"

The old preacher hit upon a mighty truth. Words are like rocks. In the hands of a David they hit the mark; in unskilled hands they go wide of it.

So it is with an effective speaker. He does not deliver the speech with his voice alone, but also with his face, eyes, hands, intellect, emotions, and personality. He is communicating to the eyes as well as the ears of the audience.

Two important considerations for improving your delivery are vocal communication and bodily communication. Let's examine each of them briefly.

Vocal Communication

The voice enables a speaker to express verbal messages and feelings to others. Many persons believe that the tone and quality of their voices are inherent with them and cannot be changed. In most cases, this is not true. With desire and by concentrated practice, one can control and change the sound of his voice. Often, merely learning to breathe properly can make a noticeable change in voice quality.

However, quality and tone of voice are not the critical parts of vocal communication. The way the voice is used is what directly helps or detracts from a speech. Some examples of those who use the voice poorly are—

1. *The yeller*, the speaker who begins his speech with a rumble, goes on with a shout, and ends with a roar, until the nerves and ears of those in the audience are exhausted.

2. *The sing-song*, the speaker who speaks with a kind of calm, rhythmic flow until his voice becomes a lullaby to many in the audience.

3. *The monotone*, the speaker whose voice never rises and falls, and who delivers his message in a flat, colorless, expressionless fashion.

A speech professor once told his students, "Begin low, go slow, rise higher, take fire, wax warm, sit down in a storm!"

Just as an animated conversation is characterized with variety in pitch, volume, and rate, so is a good speech. Pitch refers to the rising and dropping of the voice inflection; volume, to loudness and softness; and rate, to the speed at which one talks.

A good speaker varies pitch, volume, and rate to command the attention and retain the interest of the audience. Pause also may be used effectively to communicate important ideas. Pausing before and after important ideas can give meaning, emotion, and impact, and can be used to indicate where marks of punctuation might occur if you were writing instead of speaking.

Important to your vocal communication is your personality. An audience will forgive almost anything in a speaker except a lack of enthusiasm and vitality. Ralph Waldo Emerson said, "Nothing important was ever accomplished without enthusiasm." If you are exhilarated with the ideas you are expressing, your listeners will become excited also. Earnestness, fervency, intensity, and zeal have rightfully earned a place in good speaking.

Akin to enthusiasm is conviction. No speaker is more persuasive than when he speaks from the heart. If you really believe the gospel, then *speak* as if you believe it. An old preacher once remarked, "The power to convince and persuade consists of oneself being convinced and persuaded."

As you radiate enthusiasm and conviction, you will radiate confidence and friendliness. One of the surest ways to destroy the goodwill of an audience is to adopt an air of superiority or a frankness that is inappropriate. As you share your excitement and convictions in a tactful, courteous, enthusiastic way, your audience will sense your attitude and be inspired.

Bodily Communication

You can add to the convincing quality of your speech and give it life through using appropriate bodily actions. However, they must come naturally and spontaneously. Don't gesture merely to be gesturing. Gesture only for emphasis when it seems comfortable and needed. Practice using more gestures in your normal, daily conversation; then continue using hand gestures in a conversational way as you speak in public. However, at the pulpit, hand gestures must be firm and high enough to be seen. They should be used only if they can be done with confidence.

Perhaps the following descriptions will help you avoid peculiar mannerisms and gestures that distract from pulpit speaking.

1. *The hand wringer* clasps his hands, squeezing one and then the other, as he makes his points.

2. *The hair dresser* is constantly brushing his hair back and rearranging it, afraid it might be out of place.

3. *The mannequin* stands motionless with his hands at his sides and makes no movement at all. All that is needed to complete the picture is a price tag on the lapel of his coat!

The eyes are a key means of establishing contact and confidence between people. Never underestimate the power of direct eye contact in expressing sincere conviction. Train yourself to see individuals in the audience, not just a collection of bodies. Look directly into individual faces, not over heads. Many who have spoken in church recall times when someone has said, "I know you meant that for me because you looked straight at me."

Eye contact is possible only when you are thoroughly familiar with the ideas, examples, stories, and even specific wording of your talk. Glance only momentarily at your notes, or occasionally read a scripture or quotation.

Eye contact will help you establish personal relationships with your listeners, resulting in their being more interested in and involved with your message. It will give you greater confidence and help you gauge reactions, judge responses, and determine how well the audience is following your words. If you detect pleased attention, you will respond with greater enthusiasm and encouragement, and your delivery will be improved.

As you concentrate on looking directly into the faces of your listeners, remember they are looking into your face too. Therefore, your face should reflect the true meaning of what you are saying. Smiling constantly during a speech on repentance would detract from the seriousness of the subject. Likewise, frowning or appearing to be expressionless will not uplift your audience.

Dr. Charles H. Spurgeon, an effective preacher, once said, in talking to young ministers about the importance of facial expressions, "When you speak of heaven, let your face light up, let it be irradiated by a heavenly gleam, let your eyes shine with reflected glory, but when you speak of hell, your ordinary expression will do."

Good posture also helps create a good impression. Avoid lounging over the pulpit. Stand up on both feet in such a way as to command the respect of the audience, and let your hands rest lightly on the pulpit, leaving them free to make appropriate gestures. A good position in which to stand is upright with your feet in the shape of a V, the left one being slightly forward. This provides good balance and makes it possible to shift your weight from one foot to another, thus avoiding fatigue.

Important also to good communication is the proper use of a microphone. Generally the best speaking distance from the microphone is 12 to 18 inches. Learn to avoid unwanted noises that a microphone will pick up, such as breathing heavily, touching the microphone, or rustling your papers, since a sensitive instrument may pick up even the tiniest sounds. Be careful of your articulation, watching such sounds as *s*, *th*, *f*, *sh*, and their voiced equivalents, such as *z* and *zh*. Microphones exaggerate the hissing quality of these sounds.

Do not position the microphone too high, for it may block the audience's view of your face.

Stage Fright

As a television camera focuses on players prior to a football game, it is common to see some of them chewing gum, rubbing their hands, doing warm-ups, or nervously looking around. Many participants in athletic events or on the stage confess there is a keyed-up time of nervousness and fright before their performance.

Church speakers likewise experience pangs of stage fright and nervousness. A teenager named Judy had prepared diligently for her first church talk, but at the last minute she became frightened and said she was ill. Finally, with some persuasion from her parents, she gave her talk. Afterwards she confessed that it was the worry beforehand that was so terrible, but after she began her talk, the fear left her.

This is an experience familiar to many church speakers. Some have lost valuable growth experiences when they have refused to speak because of stage fright.

What causes stage fright, and how can you overcome it? Stage fright is a normal, natural condition of those who perform publicly or do anything difficult or foreign to them. Actually, it is a blessing, not a handicap, for it indicates a flow of adrenalin through the system that keys up the speaker and gives him the energy to do his best. The Lord said, ". . . if ye are prepared ye shall not fear." (D&C 38:30.) That is the key to conquering fear. If you have prepared well, prayed for strength, exercised faith, and are motivated by a positive attitude and love for your audience, you will understand and draw great comfort from the Savior's statement. If you believe what you are saying and sincerely want to convince others in a prayerful and prepared way, your nervousness will disappear as you progress in your talk.

Remember as you stand at the pulpit that you are experiencing what every speaker, actor, entertainer, or sports figure has been through many times. You can help alleviate your fears by selecting a worthwhile subject and keeping your mind on your speech rather than on yourself. Remember also the words of Franklin D. Roosevelt: "Let me assert my firm belief that the only thing we have to fear is fear itself."

Communication of God's truths in the form of speech places a great responsibility on every speaker. Each listener has the right to expect understanding, inspiration, and encouragement, and each speaker has the duty to learn the principles of good preaching. As your knowledge and delivery touch your listeners, you will find that "he that preacheth and he that receiveth, understand one another, and both are edified and rejoice together." (D&C 50:22.)

CHAPTER 14

A Speech
for Study

We have studied the step-by-step makings of a speech; now let's look at a sample speech, "Faith in Action." This speech is not intended to be an example of a perfect speech. However, it will prove helpful for analysis, particularly in illustrating the use of supporting material. The body of the speech follows a topical arrangement, using personal experience, scriptures, stories, and quotations.

Notice the directness of the language and the simplicity of the examples. The speaker introduces the subject with a personal experience, to warm up the audience. He defines terms ("what is faith?") and then moves to the heart of the talk ("faith is action"), using examples from scriptures and modern life. He concludes with a suggestion of how to make the message viable in the lives of his listeners.

In studying the sample speech, consider the differences between the written and the spoken word. The reader absorbs at his leisure with time to reread. The hearer must absorb the message in one hearing. Therefore, the speaker must repeat concepts, be specific, and use voice, facial expression, and gestures as well as words.

Faith in Action

(INTRODUCTORY STORY)

I was a teenager, active in church, and with a firm testimony of Joseph Smith. One spring afternoon, I walked to the public library to begin research for a seminary talk on Porter Rockwell. I found what I was seeking—a documented book on the very subject. I eagerly poured over the pages until the shock of what I was reading stopped me cold.

Here was a book declaring that Joseph Smith was a drunkard and Porter Rockwell a murderer! To this day, I can relive the sickening feeling that came over me. I knew the information must be false because of the teachings of my parents and church leaders. Yet, as a teenage boy with no previous exposure to anti-Mormon literature, I found myself doubting my own testimony. For that moment, my faith was being tested.

Then I remembered my grandfather's testimony of these two men, and I vowed to investigate further. I learned that Porter Rockwell was, in fact, a great obstacle to the enemies of the Church. He was imprisoned for nearly a year because of his beliefs. He managed to escape and traveled more than two hundred miles over snow and ice to see his dear prophet.

Porter arrived in Nauvoo on Christmas day, as one hundred persons were gathered in the Smith home for a banquet. Into this joyful party walked Porter, looking like a beggar of the lowest sorts. As people stared at him, he pretended to be drunk and was ordered out. The Prophet Joseph, being very well-built, decided to throw him out personally. As he took hold of this beggar, he looked into Rockwell's eyes and recognized his faithful friend. Joseph had tears in his eyes as he embraced Porter. This was the true Porter Rockwell, a man of faith—faith in the church and faith in a prophet of God.

As I read this story of faith in action, my testimony and my own faith as a teenager were renewed and strengthened.

(POINT #1—SCRIPTURE)

Today, many years later, I know that one of the greatest

assets we can possess is faith in self, country, and family—faith to live the gospel, faith in our leaders, faith in friends, and faith in God. The Lord has told us that "faith is the substance of things hoped for, the evidence of things not seen." (Hebrews 11:1.)

(QUOTATION)

Joseph Smith once said, "Faith, then, is the first great governing principle which has power, dominion, and authority over all things." (Lecture on Faith 1.) So we learn that it takes faith to believe, achieve, create, and live.

(THEME)

We might do well to change the title of this talk from "Faith in Action" to "Faith *Is* Action," for that is what we find as we learn about the principle of faith.

(QUOTATION)

James E. Talmage in *Jesus the Christ* explains that "passive belief is . . . insufficient; only when it is vitalized into active faith is it a power." (Page 319.)

(POINT #2—EXAMPLES)

The history of Christianity is replete with existing stories of active faith. It was by faith that Noah built an ark in obedience to God. It was by faith that Abraham was willing to offer up his son Isaac as a sacrifice. It was by faith that Moses led the children of Israel out of Egypt and through the Red Sea. It was by faith that Daniel was protected in the lion's den. It was by faith that David killed the giant Goliath.

(EXAMPLE)

Modern-day examples are just as forceful as ancient ones. President Spencer W. Kimball illustrates faith in action. He has suffered enough physical afflictions to try the faith of any man. Yet he has endured with no bitterness, but only greater faith and desire to serve the Almighty.

President Kimball knows the meaning of faith—action. His plea to "lengthen our stride" has gone out to the far corners of the world. His pace and dedication to work have brought new life and commitment to members and nonmembers alike. He leads the way and calls on everyone to truly make faith an action word.

(STORY)

A few years ago, a young couple who were expecting their first child were told that the young mother-to-be had a rare blood disease that was damaging the unborn baby. The team of physicians informed the heartsick couple that the young woman had no other choice but to take a certain medication that would possibly deform the fetus. The mother refused the medication, but the pain was so intense she was bedridden. Her bishop enlisted the help of the ward members, who fasted and prayed for her, exercising their faith.

Then the bishop and the husband laid their hands on her head and blessed her that she would be healed and bear a normal child. Within three weeks the painful disease was gone, and six months later, the young couple became the parents of a baby daughter, whom the pediatrician described as "one of the healthiest babies I have seen." Here were church members who made faith an action word.

Sometimes our prayers are not answered in the way we think they should be. Sometimes they are not answered according to our desires, so we experience a trial of our faith. To maintain unwavering trust in God regardless of how our prayers are answered is also faith in action.

(STORY)

Major Jay R. Jensen, a U.S. prisoner of war in Vietnam, is another example of faith in action. He suffered all types of punishment, torture, and deprivation for six years. He said, "My experience was very hard, a great test of my faith. The torture, the solitary confinement, not receiving word from my family for over three years, not being able to write and let them know I was alive—these were almost unbearable."

Then he continued, "I learned a great lesson from my experiences as a POW. That lesson is to love and appreciate the Lord and my country. I grew to appreciate my religion more. It gave me great strength that some other men did not have."

(EXAMPLES)

I recall examples of faith in action in my own home. My parents started their family of six while my father was still going to school. Money was very tight in those early years, but a full tithing was always paid. I recall the faith my mother had in the priesthood to heal her body of her many physical afflictions. I recall the faith my father had as a bishop when he helped heal sick families, physically and spiritually, and when he gave faith to those who had lost loved ones in death.

I recall my parent's teachings, their faith in action, and how they planted the seed of faith in my early life and then constantly nourished that seed.

(ANALOGY)

Developing and increasing our faith is a simple process, but it requires constant and diligent work. My son asked me one day, "Daddy, what is faith?" I believe he got a pretty good idea when we planted a garden with seeds of corn, carrots, and zucchini. He helped plant and take care of the garden and learned that a delicious vegetable will grow from a tiny seed if it is properly cared for.

Alma used a similar analogy to describe faith. He likened the gospel to a seed, which, after being planted, must be cared for and nourished if it is to bring forth fruit. One must nourish his testimony by living gospel teachings. Likewise one must nourish and care for the seed of faith, if it is to grow and wax strong.

(POINT #3)

Faith grows by following two basic steps: studying the gospel and keeping the commandments.

Faith comes by learning about Jesus Christ. His life is filled with beautiful stories of faith. On many occasions, those with great faith were healed at his hands. The New Testament tells us of the little girl whom Jesus restored to life, the nobleman's son who was healed, and Lazarus, who was miraculously raised.

The faith of Peter, the apostle, grew through his association with the Savior to the point where he could walk on water. He faltered physically only when his faith faltered.

One cannot study the gospel consistently without increasing his faith and determination to live the gospel.

The second step in nourishing the seed of faith is to keep the commandments. Once two boys were playing in a pasture when a bull started to chase them. They had been taught to ask God for help when in difficulty. One boy said, "Let's kneel and pray." The other boy said, "Let's run and pray." That is faith in action! As we obey the word of God, we become more converted and more resilient to sin. We are able to resist temptations more easily.

(EXAMPLE)

A prime example is that of Joseph of Egypt, who was tempted by his master's wife to commit adultery. Joseph was true to his faith in God and to his convictions and knowledge. He said, "How can I do this great wickedness and sin against God?"

How often have we heard the scripture, "Faith without works is dead"? How vital that knowledge is!

(EXAMPLE)

If faith means action, then action means keeping the commandments. Perhaps the greatest example of faith in action is the story of Joseph Smith as he went into the woods to pray. Because of his great faith, the Father and Son appeared to him in the flesh and gave him the great stewardship of leading the restored church of Jesus Christ.

(SCRIPTURE)

When James wrote the words that sent Joseph Smith into the woods to pray, he said, "But let him ask in faith, nothing wavering. For he that wavereth is like a wave of the sea driven with the wind and tossed." (James 1:6.)

Throughout his ministry Jesus taught the people lessons of unwavering faith. He told them to believe, and to believe implicitly. He scolded them when he said, "O ye of little faith." He encouraged them and acknowledged their devotion when he said, "Thy faith hath made thee whole." As he taught them to pray it was with the admonition, "believe that ye shall receive."

(EXAMPLES)

To study the strength of our faith, let us examine our works and our actions and see to what extent we need to build our faith. Having faith in Jesus Christ gives us the power that causes action and enables us to pray, serve others, attend church, meet trials, resist temptation, and pay our tithes.

(CONCLUSION—APPEAL)

As we consider the level of our faith, let us determine to seek greater knowledge, keep the commandments, and change passive belief into active faith. As our faith develops, we will enjoy a greater understanding of the purpose of life, a greater ability to resist temptation and live the commandments, and a greater peace of mind in days of trial.

Let us remember that without faith, nothing of worth can be accomplished. With faith, all things are possible. Faith is the first principle of the gospel because it is faith that gives us the motivation and power to do things we must in order to be saved.

May we have the faith to create and contribute. May we increase our faith in the gospel of Jesus Christ, faith in church leaders, faith in our country, and most of all, faith in ourselves, I pray in the name of Jesus Christ. Amen.

CHAPTER 15

Using the Scriptures

Preparation for a talk on any gospel subject is not complete until you have consulted the standard works to find out what the Lord has said on the subject.

Scripture is the word of God, not only to people of past generations, but to the world today. Through scripture study, one can get closer to the Lord and learn about his eternal plan, for he has told us: ". . . out of the books which shall be written I will judge the world, every man according to their works, according to that which is written." (2 Nephi 29:11.) In our own dispensation, he has said, "Behold, I say unto you that you shall let your time be devoted to the studying of the scriptures. . . ." (D&C 26:1.)

In studying the scriptures, read carefully with a purpose and a desire to learn. Study prayerfully with reverence and faith. If possible, try to put yourself into the historical and cultural setting about which you are reading. Create mental pictures in your mind as you read—imagining how the characters look and the settings and situations involved.

Remember, the books of scripture should not be read as textbooks. They are religious records that reveal God's dealings with man. They are guides to everyday living and source books for developing faith in the reality of God and Christ, and understanding of their eternal plan.

Prayerfully search the scriptures in order to understand the intent and spirit of the author of each book of scripture, and try to read with the same spirit of faith, humility, and reverence with which he wrote.

Look for beauty of expression and the way in which thoughts are expressed. Feed the soul as well as the intellect.

Keep in mind that study of the scriptures does not imply blind, unthinking acceptance. As the closing chapter of the Book of Mormon recommends, every reader should seek confirmation from God as to the value and truth of the record. (See Moroni 10:3-17.)

The Savior has told us that the scriptures should be searched: "And now, behold, I say unto you, that ye ought to search these things. Yea, a commandment I give unto you that ye search these things diligently. . . ." (3 Nephi 23:1.) Nephi tells us that we should feast upon the word of Christ, for therein will we have eternal life. (See 2 Nephi 31:20.)

Understanding the Scriptures

Before you use the scriptures effectively in any talk or lesson, you must first be able to discern and understand well the message. In 2 Peter we read, ". . . no prophecy of the scripture is of any private interpretation. For the prophecy came not in old time by the will of man: but holy men of God spake as they were moved by the Holy Ghost." (2 Peter 1:20-21.)

You can explain a scripture only after you have prayed for spiritual guidance in understanding it. Then compare and verify your interpretation with written statements of the prophets of the Church and in light of official Church policies. If you still have questions concerning your interpretation, go to your bishop or branch president for guidance.

To help you better understand a scripture, read not only the verse you may wish to quote, but also the entire chapter in which it appears. A mistake many speakers make is in quoting a scripture out of context, which may actually make the information inaccurate. Be sure you do not detract from the general purpose and theme of the context in which it occurs.

It is helpful to cross-reference scriptural passages with other books in the standard works, commentaries by Church writers, and footnotes that occur in the scriptural text.

Avoid making generalizations and broad doctrinal conclusions on the basis of only a small fraction of evidence. An example of this would be the scriptural phrase "Go, and do thou likewise." (Luke 10:37.) This phrase was given in a specific context by the Savior in telling the parable of the Good Samaritan, and should not be used as a general admonition for a dissimilar situation.

The Witness of the Holy Spirit

The key to understanding the scriptures is found in the witness of the Holy Spirit. The Prophet Joseph Smith left us this formula of discernment:

I have a key by which I understand the scriptures. I enquire, what was the question which drew out the answer, or caused Jesus to utter the parable? . . . . To ascertain its meaning, we must dig up the root and ascertain what it was that drew the saying out of Jesus. (Teachings of the Prophet Joseph Smith, *pp. 276-77.*)

When Joseph Smith and Oliver Cowdery were baptized in May 1829, according to the Prophet,

We were filled with the Holy Ghost, and rejoiced in the God of our salvation.

Our minds being now enlightened, we began to have the scriptures laid open to our understandings, and the true meaning and intention of their more mysterious passages revealed unto us in a manner which we never could attain to previously, nor ever before had thought of. . . . (Joseph Smith 2:73-74.)

One must have the Spirit in order to gain understanding of the scriptures. This is the substance of a passage in the Doctrine and Covenants:

Therefore, why is it that ye cannot understand and know, that he that receiveth the word by the Spirit of truth receiveth it as it is preached by the Spirit of truth?

Wherefore, he that preacheth and he that receiveth, understand one another, and both are edified and rejoice together. (D&C 50:21-22.)

Paul also explained this to the saints at Corinth, when he contrasted the spirit of man with the Spirit of God:

. . . God hath revealed them unto us by his Spirit: for the Spirit searcheth all things, yea, the deep things of God.

80

For what man knoweth the things of a man, save the spirit of man which is in him? even so the things of God knoweth no man, but the Spirit of God.

Now we have received, not the spirit of the world, but the spirit which is of God; that we might know the things that are freely given to us of God.

Which things also we speak, not in the words which man's wisdom teacheth, but which the Holy Ghost teacheth; comparing spiritual things with spiritual.

But the natural man receiveth not the things of the Spirit of God: for they are foolishness to him: neither can he know them, because they are spiritually discerned. (1 *Corinthians 2:10-14.*)

Application to a Talk in Church

Now, having searched the scriptures, studied them out in your mind, prayed about them, and received the witness of the Holy Spirit, how do you use them in your talk?

First of all, wherever possible, give a brief explanation of the context, background, or setting in which they appear.

Cite the source properly; i.e., "Moroni, chapter 10, verse 3," not "Moroni 10 and 3."

Avoid reading long passages; audience concentration is generally quite low, particularly when a speaker is reading something. Remember the great importance of eye contact. If you do use scriptures, try to know them well enough so you can look at your audience occasionally. Speak clearly and with feeling.

Do not use verses or parts of verses that do not contribute or are not relevant to your subject.

Scripture-reading is more effective if you can read directly from the standard works and not from a typewritten or handwritten copy. Mark the scriptures so you can turn to them easily during your talk. Practice handling the book and verbally rehearsing your reading.

State how each particular scripture is to be applied, such as (1) to reinforce a theme, (2) to verify a gospel truth, (3) to teach by example, (4) to tell a story, or (5) to build faith or give comfort.

And lastly, share your conviction and testimony of the truthfulness of the scriptures you read. Where appropriate, share personal experiences to illustrate their importance.

Here are some selected stories, sermons, and parables from the scriptures that might be used as the basis for your talk. In parentheses after each source are gospel applications.

Bible Stories

Creation—Genesis 1:1-31, 2:1-3 (power of God; divine order; keeping the Sabbath day holy)

Fall of man—Genesis 3 (obedience)

Cain and Abel—Genesis 4:1-15 (jealousy; pride)

Noah and the flood—Genesis 6:5, 9:17 (wickedness; power of God; trust in God; an act of love)

Tower of Babel—Genesis 11:1-9 (God's dealings with wickedness)

Abraham and Lot—Genesis 13:5-18 (unselfishness)

Sacrifice of Isaac—Genesis 22:1-19 (faith in God; obedience)

Isaac and Rebecca—Genesis 24:1-67 (prayer; faith; marriage in the covenant)

Esau sells his birthright—Genesis 24:21-34 (ideals; perseverance)

Jacob and Rachel—Genesis 29:1-30 (endurance; patience)

Joseph—Genesis 37-45 (freedom comes by obedience)

Birth of Moses—Exodus 2:1-10, 1:7-14 (God fulfills his purposes even when men's weaknesses seem to make it difficult)

Pillar of cloud—Exodus 13:17-22 (God will guide his children)

Passage through the Red Sea—Exodus 14:5-6, 10:31 (God will protect his children and fight their battles; faith)

Golden calf—Exodus 32:1-24 (we should be steadfast, believing, and not doubt when things don't appear to be going well)

Balaam—Numbers 22, 23, 24:1-38 (obedience)

Fall of Jericho—Joshua 6:1-7, 10-11, 14-17, 20 (God will guide his children)

Deborah and Jael—Judges 4:4-22 (when God's servants speak, we should pay attention)

Gideon and the three hundred—Judges 7:1-22; 8:1-4 (God can accomplish great things against seemingly great odds)

Jotham and the trees—Judges 9:7-16 (supporting our leaders)

Samson and Delilah—Judges 16:4-30 (avoiding temptation)

Ruth—Ruth (faithfulness and loyalty)

Call of Samuel—1 Samuel 3:1-10 (heed the voice of the Lord; follow priesthood leaders)

Samuel meets Saul—1 Samuel 9-10 (God selects leaders according to his wisdom, not man's)

David and Goliath—1 Samuel 17:20-54 (faith in God; cause greater than self)

David and Jonathan—1 Samuel 20:18-23 (brotherhood)

Saul and the witch of Endor—1 Samuel 28:7-25 (justice and punishment)

Nathan's reproof of David—2 Samuel 12:1-10 (secret acts are known to God)

Solomon's choice of wisdom—1 Kings 3:5-15 (seek God-like qualities)

Judgments by Solomon—1 Kings 3:16-28 (necessity of seeking wisdom)

Solomon and the Queen of Sheba—1 Kings 10:1-13 (example of righteousness)

Elijah and the prophets of Baal—1 Kings 18:1-46 (faith in God)

Elijah and Elisha—2 Kings 2:1-25 (power of God)

Elijah and Naaman—2 Kings 5:1-19 (faith in God)

Esther—Esther (loyalty; power of fasting and prayer)

Ezekiel's vision of the resurrection—Ezekiel 37 (resurrection and redemption)

Ezekiel's redemption of Judah; healing of the Dead Sea—Ezekiel 47 (redemption of Judah; promises fulfilled)

Daniel—Daniel (faith)

Jonah—Jonah (obedience and disobedience; God's love is universal)

Birth of Christ—Matthew 1:18-25, Luke 2:1-39 (fulfillment of prophecy; kindness of God the Father)

Visit of the wise men—Matthew 2:1-12 (worship)

Flight into Egypt—Matthew 2:13-21 (how God protects his children)

Death of John the Baptist—Matthew 14, Mark 6 (faithfulness to the end; martyrdom; testimony sealed with blood)

Mount of Transfiguration—Matthew 17, Luke 9, Mark 9 (keys of the kingdom in the meridian of time)

Death of Jesus—Matthew 26, 27 (atonement)

Resurrection of Jesus—Matthew 28, John 17 (power over death; redemption)

Birth of John—Luke 1:5-80 (power of God)

Jesus in the temple—Luke 2:1-51 (Christ's divine Sonship)

Jesus heals a blind man—John 9 (power of Jesus; love of Jesus for people)

Jesus raises Lazarus from the dead—John 11 (Jesus' power over death)

Old Testament Parables

Trees making a king (Jotham)—Judges 9:7-15 (supporting our leaders)

Samson's riddle to marriage guests—Judges 14:14 (deception; dishonesty; keeping promises)

Poor man's ewe lamb (Nathan)—2 Samuel 12:1-31 (greed; selfishness)

Woman of Tekoah—2 Samuel 14:6-11 (accountability of parents)

Escaped prisoner—1 Kings 20:35-40 (law of justice; inevitable judgments)

Vision of Micaiah—1 Kings 22:19-23 (false prophets)

The drunkard—Proverbs 23:29-35 (subtle and evil effects of alcohol; judge not by first appearances)

Sluggard and his vineyard—Proverbs 24:30-34 (devastating effects of laziness; how one can lose wealth little by little)

Unfruitful vineyard—Isaiah 5:1-6 (woes to the wicked; pride)

Plowman—Isaiah 28:23-29 (a sure foundation in Zion)

Great eagles and the vine—Ezekiel 17:3-10 (importance of keeping covenants; God will make the least great)

Lion's whelps—Ezekiel 23 (judgment against immorality)

Boiling pot—Ezekiel 24:3-5 (purging of the wicked)

Cedar in Lebanon—Ezekiel 31 (greatness and glory come through living the commandments)

Sea monster—Ezekiel 32:1-18 (cursing and sorrow for the wicked)

Shepherds and the flock—Ezekiel 34 (selfishness; necessity of service and charity)

New Testament Parables

Tares—Matthew 12:24-30 (all men should cultivate patience, long-suffering, tolerance; righteous and wicked will receive just rewards)

Hidden treasures—Matthew 13:44 (be willing to sacrifice all you have to retain treasures of heaven)

Pearl of great price—Matthew 13:45-46 (search persistently for truth, and be willing to sacrifice all to possess it)

Gospel net—Matthew 13:47 (all men are to be judged good from bad; all die, but not alike)

Unmerciful servant—Matthew 18:23-34 (forgiveness)

Laborers in the vineyard—Matthew 21:28-32 (unconditional service; indebtedness to God)

Two sons—Matthew 21:28-32 (hypocrisy; repentance)

Royal marriage feast—Matthew 22:1-14 (many called but few chosen; salvation through doing the word)

Ten virgins—Matthew 25:1-13 (preparedness)

Talents—Matthew 25:14-30 (faithfulness; service)

Sheep and goats—Matthew 25:31-46 (certainty of judgment)

Seed growing secretly—Mark 4:26-29 (sowers of God's word do so humbly, without public attention; humility; faith; hope)

Household watching—Mark 13:34-37 (preparing for the second coming)

Two debtors—Luke 7:36-50 (forgiveness)

Good Samaritan—Luke 10:25-37 (brotherhood; charity)

Friend at midnight—Luke 11:5-8 (persistence brings results)

Foolish rich man—Luke 12:16-21 (selfishness; hypocrisy)

Servants watching—Luke 12:35-40 (contrast between faithful and wicked)

Steward on trial—Luke 12:42-43 (accountability for stewardship)

Barren fig tree—Luke 13:6-9 (hypocrisy)

Great supper—Luke 14:16-24 (opportunities won or lost)

Tower of the warring king—Luke 14:28-33 (count the costs before undertaking a task)

Importunate widow—Luke 18:2-5 (pray and do not faint)

Lost coin—Luke 15:8-10 (repentance; worth of souls)

Prodigal son—Luke 15:11-32 (worth of a soul; repentance; faithfulness; devotion)

Unrighteous steward—Luke 16:1-13 (striving for spiritual wealth)

Rich man and Lazarus—Luke 16:19-31 (danger in dependence on man; relationship of mortal life to life after death)

Unprofitable servants—Luke 17:7-10 (going the extra mile; sacrifice)

Pharisee and publican—Luke 18:9-14 (self-righteousness; humility)

Pounds—Luke 19:12-27 (service; talent)

Bread of life—John 6 (salvation and eternal life through Christ)

Shepherd and sheep—John 10 (safety in following Christ)

Vine and branches—John 15 (relationship of Christ to his followers; personal growth through Christ)

House built on rock and on sand—Matthew 7:24-29; Luke 6:48-49 (revelation; building proper foundations)

Leaven—Matthew 13:33; Luke 13:20 (truth and good stimulate one from within to rise to great heights; the effect of testimony)

Lost sheep—Matthew 18:12; Luke 15 (saving purpose of Christ's mission; worth of a soul)

Candle under a bushel—Matthew 5; Mark 4; Luke 8 (example; talents)

New cloth on old garments—Matthew 9; Mark 2; Luke 5 (newness and completeness of gospel)

New wine in old bottles—Matthew 9; Mark 2; Luke 5 (newness and completeness of gospel)

Sower—Matthew 13; Mark 4; Luke 8 (preparation and endurance; various reactions to the gospel)

Widow's mite—Mark 12:41-44; Luke 21:1-4 (sacrifice; giving one's all)

Mustard seed—Matthew 13:31-32; Mark 4:31-32; Luke 13:18-19 (seed of truth begins small, but grows to encompass all)

Vineyard and husbandmen—Matthew 21; Mark 12; Luke 20 (rejecting righteousness; selfishness)

Young leaves of the figtree—Matthew 24; Mark 13; Luke 21 (signs of the times tell nearness of the second coming)

Sermons from the Bible

Christ—Matthew 5-7; John 10:1-18 (the good Shepherd; Sermon on the Mount; Beatitudes)

Christ—John 14-16 (perfect law of love; two comforters; mission of the Holy Ghost)

Isaiah—Isaiah 55, 61 (listen to the Lord; God's ways are not man's; joy through Christ)

Isaiah—Isaiah 58:1-11 (proper reasons for fasting)

Joshua—Joshua 24:15-24 (choose whom you will serve)

Moses—Deuteronomy 30:11-20 (men judged righteously; God is final judge)

Peter—Acts 2:14-40 (testimony of Jesus Christ)

Peter—Acts 3:1-26 (power of priesthood; faith; repentance; testimony of Christ)

Peter—Acts 4:1-12 (Jesus Christ—the only true Savior)

Stephen—Acts 7 (divine heritage; prophets of old; miracles of God)

Paul—Acts 13:16-41 (resurrection; forgiveness)

Paul—Acts 17:16-34 (ignorance of things of God)

Paul—Acts 22:1-21, 26 (Paul's testimony of Christ)

Book of Mormon Stories

Nephi secures brass plates—1 Nephi 3, 4 (God helps men accomplish his will)

Lehi's dream of the tree—1 Nephi 8, 15 (obedience to God's word; help through the journeys of life)

Liahona—1 Nephi 16:10, 27-28; 18:12-24 (faith)

Tame and wild olive trees—Jacob 5, 6 (enduring to the end; inevitable judgment; a philosophy of history)

Sherem—Jacob 7:1-20 (deathbed repentance; sign-seeking)

Enos' prayer—Enos 1-8 (repentance; forgiveness)

Conversion of Alma the younger—Mosiah 27 (power of parental prayers)

Sons of Mosiah and their missions—Mosiah 28:1-10; Alma 17-26 (true repentance; mercy of God)

The Lord makes the bondage light, and his people return to Zarahemla—Mosiah 24 (devotion to God; courage; mercy of God)

Amlici seeks to become king—Alma 2 (cunning of the wicked)

Zeezrom confounded by Amulek—Alma 11:20-46; 15:1-12 (power of testimony)

Amulek and Alma—Alma 11-15 (plan of redemption; love of God)

Ammon and his mission—Alma 17-20 (companionship of the Holy Ghost)

Conversion of King Lamoni—Alma 18, 19 (teaching by the Spirit)

Repentant Lamanites submit to slaughter rather than risk committing sin—Alma 24 (repentance)

Korihor says there is no God—Alma 30:12-60 (flatteries of man; evidences of God)

Alma to his sons—Alma 36-40 (wise counsel from a patient father)

Greatness of Moroni the patriot—Alma 48 (being a saint and a soldier)

Alma's last blessing and departure—Alma 45:1-19 (a father's blessing)

Helaman and his two thousand warriors—Alma 56:9-57 (God strengthens the righteous)

Abinadi—Mosiah 11-17 (divine protection)

Conversion of Alma the elder—Mosiah 17 (courage to stand for the right)

King Noah sends an army to destroy Alma—Mosiah 18-19, 24 (trust in the Lord; divine protection)

Nephites repent and escape from enemies—Mosiah 21-22 (repentance)

Brothers encircled by fire; Lamanites repent—Helaman 5:14-52 (repentance; faith)

Samuel the Lamanite—Helaman 13-15 (prophecy and testimony of Christ)

Signs of the Savior's birth—3 Nephi 1:1-19 (prophecy fulfilled; Christlike compassion)

Nephi's power of faith raises his brother to life—3 Nephi 7:15-20 (faith)

Christ's crucifixion attested by predicted signs—3 Nephi 8-9 (prophecy and judgment)

Jesus Christ comes to the Nephites—3 Nephi 11-28 (baptism; Beatitudes; prayer; law of Christ)

Three Nephites—3 Nephi 28:1-24; Mormon 8:10-11 (desire to serve; unselfishness; sacrifice)

Church flourishes for two hundred years—4 Nephi (effects of righteousness)

Ammaron's charge to Mormon—Mormon 1 (importance of recordkeeping; God's trust in youth)

Impenitent Nephite race destroyed like Jaredites—Mormon 1-8 (repentance)

Moroni, the lone survivor—Mormon 8; Moroni 10:2, 34 (enduring to the end; atonement and repentance)

Jared and his brother—Ether 1:33; 6 (faith in God)
Downfall of the Jaredite nation through refusal to heed warnings—
Ether 12, 14-15 (compare 2:9-12) (repentance)

Book of Mormon Parables

Abinadi—Mosiah 12:10-12 (parable-like expressions showing weakness of a wicked man)
Alma—Alma 32 (faith is like a seed)
Alma—Alma 37:38-45 (parable-like comparison of the Liahona and true life)
Moroni—Alma 46:23-27 (parable-like comparison of a torn garment and true experiences of life)

Book of Mormon Sermons

King Benjamin—Mosiah 2-4 (service; conditions of salvation; man's dependence on God)
Abinadi—Mosiah 15-16 (Jesus, the Father and the Son; resurrection and judgment)
Amulek—Alma 34 (atonement; prayer; repentance)
Nephi—Helaman 7-8, 10 (pride)
Samuel—Helaman 13-15 (prophecies of Christ)
Christ—3 Nephi 11-17 (baptism; Beatitudes; prayer; law of Christ)
Alma—Alma 5 (need for repentance)
Alma—Alma 7 (how to be spiritual)
Alma—Alma 9 (repentance)
Alma—Alma 12 (plan of salvation)
Alma—Alma 32 (faith)
Alma—Alma 33 (true worship)
Alma—Alma 40 (resurrection)
Alma—Alma 41 (judgment)

Doctrine and Covenants Parables

"If ye are not one, ye are not mine"—38:25-27 (brotherhood; unity)
Fig tree—45:36-38 (righteous look for signs of times)
Wheat and tares—86:1-7 (division of good and evil; responsibility of priesthood in last days)
Steward and laborers in the field—88:51-61 (seek to be near to God before he comes)

Twelve olive trees—101:43-62 (gathering of the Saints)

Widow avenged—101:83-84 (pray and not faint; Lord will deal with wicked in the end)

Ten virgins—63:54; 45:56-59 (preparing for the coming of the Lord)

Pearl of Great Price Stories

Moses and Satan—Moses 1 (overcoming Satan by faith in Jesus Christ)

Enoch—Moses 6 (anything is possible with the Lord's help)

Enoch—Moses 7:13-16 (Enoch's faith causes enemies to flee)

Abraham and his father—Abraham (succeeding in spite of a bad home environment)

Visit of the Father and Son follows prayer of faith—Joseph Smith 2:11-19 (faith; prayer)

Angel Moroni comes after prayer of faith—Joseph 2:29-43 (faith; prayer)

CHAPTER 16

Studying Church Sermons

Conference addresses may serve as excellent source material for Church talks. Reading and studying them can give you great insight, helping you develop your own thoughts, philosophy, and beliefs.

In general conference in April 1973, President Harold B. Lee declared:

If you want to know what the Lord has for this people at the present time, I would admonish you to get and read the discourses that have been delivered at this conference, for what these brethren have spoken by the power of the Holy Ghost is the mind of the Lord, the will of the Lord, the voice of the Lord, and the power of God unto salvation. (Ensign, *July 1973, p. 74.*)

The sermons delivered at general conference can serve as excellent patterns for the development of a good gospel sermon. However, in reading them, remember that it is impossible for a printed speech to reproduce the atmosphere and spirit present when it was given. Even if one has previously heard the speech delivered, it is difficult to recall, while reading the words on the printed page, the enthusiasm and conviction of the speaker's voice, the sparkle in his eyes, the glow in his face, his gestures and timely pauses. It is, therefore, important to approach reading a printed sermon in the right attitude and spirit if you want to develop a sincere appreciation for its message and add to your knowledge and understanding of the gospel.

How to Study a Conference Address

1. Preview the talk to get a broad, general idea of the message. Note the title and the name of the speaker. Then read the first two or three paragraphs, the first (topical) sentence of each succeeding paragraph, and the last two paragraphs. On a sheet of paper, write down the title of the sermon and then the general message or main idea.

2. Ask mental questions about the subject and the talk as you preview it, such as, What are the key statements? What are some of the commands or instructions that I should write down and follow?

3. Read the talk carefully and prayerfully and with a definite purpose in mind, searching for answers that may enrich your life. Resolve to profit from the talk. Weigh, consider, and evaluate how it might be applied to your life.

4. As you read, mark pertinent passages or take notes, to keep your mind alert and active. The marked talk is the thought-through talk. Underline key statements and quotable thoughts. In the margins or at the top or bottom of the page, record your reactions, questions, and ideas you can apply. Number the sequence of the author's key points. Note any significant interpretations of scriptural passages.

A Conference Talk to Study

The late Elder Richard L. Evans of the Council of the Twelve was admired by countless listeners for his inspiring messages delivered each Sunday for more than forty years in the weekly broadcast of "Music and the Spoken Word" from the Tabernacle on Temple Square. He traveled throughout the world as a General Authority and as president of Rotary International. His many books, articles, and sermons have touched the lives of countless persons.

The following sermon, "Decisions—Which Road for You?," was delivered at general conference in October 1968. It was a time of widespread violence, drug abuse, breakdown in morality, and public opposition to United States involvement in war in Viet Nam. Therefore, his message was particularly timely for parents and youth in reaffirming the importance of making the right decisions and choosing the right paths in life.

The notations in the margins are those of a reader who analyzed the talk and wrote down pertinent points. Italics indicate passages that were underlined by the reader.

Decisions—Which Road for You?

Some days ago, on September 17, as referred to by President [David O.] McKay this morning, we dedicated a new flagpole on Temple Square, with flags flying a hundred feet high and a base and background of panels on liberty and law, including the Ten Commandments and some other reminders of our basic beliefs, among them these:

"We believe that governments were instituted of God for the benefit of man; and that he holds men accountable for their acts in relation to them, both in making laws and administering them, for the good and safety of society.

"We believe that no government can exist in peace, except such laws are framed and held inviolate as will secure to each individual the free exercise of conscience, the right and control of property, and the protection of life." (D&C 134:1-2.)

"We believe in . . . obeying, honoring, and sustaining the law." (Article of Faith 12.)

Theme   Despite an all too prevalent and all too popular appeal to permissiveness, we still reap what we sow. *And I would plead this day, with the young, the old, with the counselors of youth, the teachers of youth—with all of us—to recommit ourselves to living by law.*

To those who are pulling away from God-given and long-proved principles, abandoning and protesting, may I offer the very interesting observation of a wise and seasoned president whose stake I

93

was recently privileged to visit, and who said, in substance, with golf course connotation, "When there is all that fairway, why do you play so much in the rough?" (President Rudolph L. Van Kampen, Riverdale [Utah] Stake.)

Point #1
Irresponsible protests.
This could also apply to teenagers' relationships with parents and home.

Too many are playing in the rough, frustrated, foolishly dissipating present possibilities, and jeopardizing the limitless opportunities of everlasting life. Too many are protesting, lashing out in anger, without making any constructive contribution to solving the ills and the evils. We ought to be angry about evil and never be complacent, never let it quietly seep into our surroundings. But we ought not to be angry and resentful against good advice, against reasonable restraint, against the counsels God has given. Stubborn, blind, brash anger, going ahead against all safeguards and danger signs, is an utterly shortsighted and self-destructive anger.

Let me insert here some comments on irresponsible protest from three or four significant sources, dating back to the last century and coming down to the present scene.

The first is from Phillips Brooks: "If circumstances taunt and persecute you," he said, "if everything you touch is a strain and a temptation, do not stand idly wishing that the world were changed. The change must be in you. . . . Back on the wills of men, where it belongs, falls the responsibility of sin. . . ." (*Twenty Sermons*, No. 14.)

The second, from Dr. Fosdick, comes closer to us in time: "Today, . . . I am dealing with a special area of young persons, some of whom, I think, are fooling themselves," he said. ". . . they find it easier to become excited over social reform than to deal with their own characters. . . .

"They are, for example, pacifists in general (allegedly so), but they have such a quality of spirit

94

that they break up the peace of any group they enter. . . . They ardently say that the world needs to be changed but their neighbors know that, however that may be, *they* certainly need to be changed. . . .

"Suppose that the social reforms . . . were now successfully achieved. Can anyone who . . . visualizes that redeemed society suppose that . . . personal character would be called for less? Surely, personal character would be called for more.

". . . always in history character and happiness have come to people . . . when they shouldered their personal responsibility. . . ." (Harry Emerson Fosdick, "On Shouldering One's Own Responsibility.")

The third is a comment from George Kennan (former U.S. Ambassador to Russia and Pulitzer Prize author) as recently reported:

"The revolutionary habit may get ominously out of hand. . . . Violent protest . . . amounts to 'intimidation and blackmail'; if tolerated, it leads to dictatorship. 'I have seen more harm done in this world by those who tried to storm the bastions of society in the name of utopian beliefs . . . than by all the humble efforts of those who have tried to create a little order and civility and affection within their own intimate entourage. . . .'" The revolutionaries . . . have not been able to face a 'vitally important truth'; namely, that the 'decisive seat of evil in this world is not in the social and political institutions and not even, as a rule, in the ill will or iniquities of statesmen but simply in the weakness and imperfection of the human soul itself, and by that I mean literally every soul, including my own and that of the student militant at the gate.'

"The disquieting thing about today's revolutionaries is that many of them could not care less about traditional good and evil. Their vision is apocalyptic. . . . 'Ultimately . . . it will accept nothing save . . . obliteration of all stabilities.' "

"People yearn for ultimate upheaval," said Earl Rovit, "because they believe it will restore 'innocence and purity' to the world. . . Yet it may be destruction that really attracts them. Their basic attitude is not that they 'want to break windows in order to let the fresh air in.' . . . the fact is they are 'hopelessly in love with the sound of smashing glass.' " (*Time*, June 28, 1968, p. 47; quoting Kennan and Rovit.)

Point #2
Roads &
pathways to
choose

Recently, with some much appreciated help, *I have had occasion to select some citations on the roads and pathways that people pursue:*

"Any road leads to the end of the world," said Edward Fitzgerald. (*Polonius*, p. 86.)

"Where the road bends abruptly take short steps." (Ernest Bramah.)

And, of course, there is the classic poem from Robert Frost on "The Road Not Taken."

Point #3
Don't choose
the wrong
road

My beloved young friends, let us not destroy ourselves by taking the wrong road—by refusing counsel, by departing from proved principles, by yielding to appetites, by indulging passions, by straying off the straight way that leads to life and truth and to all the limitless accomplishments of the everlasting future, as well as peace and purpose and happiness here.

Of course, the young—and all of us—are often impatient to see Utopia come sooner, to see everything set right, right now. There may be in the air a little of the feeling of Hamlet:

"The time is out of joint: O cursed spite, That ever I was born to set it right!" (William Shakespeare, *Hamlet*, Act I, sc. 5.)

But just plain protest and rebellion and dissipation and destruction will not set things right.

96

Point #4
*Noble birth.
Direct
energies
toward God*

The answer is that we were all born to set right whatever should be set right that is within our reach. We shouldn't dodge or run from duty, but should be engaged in the service of our fellowmen, in the service of the Master, in doing all that should and can be done.

Point #5
*Opportunities
in church*

And as to opportunities for action, there is in the Church of Jesus Christ provision for activity and action pertaining to the physical and mental and spiritual health and wholeness of all men everywhere. There is outlet and opportunity for the strength and service of all who wish to help toward the peace and well-being of all people: welfare, serving others, taking care of our own; tithing; teaching; health, hospitals; schools here at home; educating the less privileged in far places; bringing thousands of the children of others into our homes and hospitals; youth programs, athletics, talent development, cultural and recreational activities; rehabilitating people with problems; preserving the integrity of home and marriage and family life; caring for the sick, compassionate service; encouragement to seek knowledge, to develop skills, to acquire competence, to qualify for professional service; encouragement to be active in politics, civic affairs, public service; to foster freedom; to share the gospel, to teach the truth; to move among all peoples—to learn their languages, to become acquainted with customs and cultures; to be anxiously and constructively concerned about the physical, mental, moral, spiritual well-being, the peace and health and happiness of all people—and with the earnest intent and endeavor that all this be done without the use of public funds.

The list could be multiplied to include a completeness of provision for the temporal and eternal salvation of all.

My beloved young friends—and you who are

older: There are some things that are "not good for man" and which we are counseled not to do and not to partake of, but basically this is *not* a gospel of *not* doing. There is ample opportunity for all for the outlet of all your energy and earnest intent for the blessing and upbuilding of people at home and worldwide.

Of course the world has troubles, uncertainties, problems. Of course we are impatient and puzzled at times, but the means and the reason for improving and repenting and for solving the problems are given us in our Father's plans and purposes.

May I cite two oft-quoted scriptures, and put some added emphasis on them:

Point #6
Be engaged in
a good cause

"Verily I say, *men should be anxiously engaged in a good cause, and do many things of their own free will, and bring to pass much righteousness.*" (*D&C* 58:27.)

The emphasis could well be on *good* and *righteousness*.

Another: "Wherefore, honest men and wise men should be sought for diligently, and good men and wise men ye should observe to uphold. . . ." (D&C 98:10.)

I infer from this that we have an obligation to be active in public issues, in civic problems, and to provide honest and good men and wise men to serve and give leadership in public affairs.

We shouldn't be sideline sitters.

With you, I thank God for a prophet to guide us in these latter days. He has given us counsel at this conference, and through all his faithful years in the great-hearted kindliness and inspiration of his calling.

I hope and pray that we may accept the counsel of President McKay, and the counsel of Him whom he serves.

The Lord hasn't asked of any of us anything that we can't do, nor given us any commandment that we can't keep.

I only know one place to put my trust—in the counsels and commandments of God, which patiently he has repeated over and over through the ages, and again and again given us.

Point #7
Example

Mothers, fathers: Set before your children a righteous example. Love them; lead them. Take them where they should be. If they follow you, be sure that they follow you in the right habits, to the right places, for the right purposes. Don't lead off in any direction in which you would wish they wouldn't follow.

Point #8
Youth, choose
the right

And you, *my beloved young friends:* You have more opportunities than any generation ever had. God bless you to *choose the right, to use your energies in constructive, righteous ways,* in useful, virtuous, productive performance, not in irresponsible protest, not dropping out, but entering in, with the full use of the opportunities and talents God has given you, knowing and keeping his commandments, honoring, obeying, and sustaining and upholding the law, and going forward in faith with peace and accomplishment and quiet conscience.

"Any road leads to the end of the world."

"When there is all that fairway, why do you play so much in the rough?"

"What is the use of running when you are on the wrong road?" (W. G. Benham, *Proverbs.*)

I leave you my witness of this work, my witness of the living God who is our Father and who made us in his own image—my witness of the divinity of his beloved Son, our Lord and Savior. All he did was for the salvation of men.

Plea: positive
production

May each of us follow his example and seek with all our hearts to save ourselves, our families, and all our Father's family, to the very best of our abilities and energies and opportunities—not negatively protesting, but positively producing; not sitting down, but serving and moving forward; not destroying, but creating; not infecting with doubt, but building with faith; I pray in the name of Jesus Christ, our beloved Lord and Savior. Amen. (*Improvement Era,* December 1968, pp. 64-66.)

CHAPTER 17

How to Listen to Church Talks

"Let us be silent that we may hear the whispers of the gods." So wrote Emerson, the poet, many decades ago.

In contemporary years, the novelist Ernest Hemingway said it another way: "I like to listen; I have learned a great deal from listening carefully."

These two statements could well apply to Church members who attend many meetings each year in which their task for the most part is one of learning by listening.

Formal communication in church is a circular process. The speaker's duty is to communicate to the listener by the Spirit, and the listener's responsibility is to receive by the Spirit and then return nonverbal feedback of support and humility.

Church members should attend meetings with a desire to receive the Spirit and to learn, repent, and improve. How rare is the person who privately or with his family pauses before he leaves home to specifically ask divine help for the speakers he is about to hear!

Sometimes people blame speakers for an unfulfilling meeting, when in reality they themselves have done nothing to add spiritual strength to the speaker through silent prayers and humble listening.

To a Latter-day Saint who has sought the Spirit and then listens intently can come great gifts, including wisdom, understanding, knowledge, and faith. (See D&C 46.) Sermons may help us overcome our weaknesses and gain strength, but we must ask the Lord for his gifts in order to accomplish this.

The Lord explained this process in a revelation given through the Prophet Joseph Smith:

Therefore, why is it that ye cannot understand and know, that he that receiveth the word by the Spirit of truth receiveth it as it is preached by the Spirit of truth?

Wherefore, he that preacheth and he that receiveth, understand one another, and both are edified and rejoice together. (D&C 50:21-22.)

A mission president in Canada a few years ago stood to address a group of missionaries. He began to speak with some difficulty and then stopped.

"I will not continue my talk because the Spirit is not here," he said. "I have come prepared to have it here, but you have not come prepared for it."

Then, changing the format of the meeting, he called a few missionaries from the group to bear their testimonies and "preach the Spirit" there. Following this, he invited another missionary to lead the group in prayer, on their knees, and to "pray the Spirit" there. As the prayer was concluded, a spirit of humility came over the group and the president was able to once again stand and deliver his message.

In his talk, he explained, "You, as the listeners, must desire as intently as the speaker that this be a spiritual feasting. And you, as well as I, must come prepared to that end."

How to Become an Effective Listener

We have seen that an effective sermon consists of effective listening as well as effective speaking. How does one become a good listener?

Of significant importance is to listen with respect. You may not agree with the organization of a speech, the delivery, or even the speaker's appearance, but you can still listen with kindness and courtesy. Listening is tied in part to loving. If one is basically heedless of a speaker, he is apt to be heedless of his words. To listen with understanding is to try to put oneself in tune with the speaker and his message, to become involved, interested, concerned, and to listen with the heart.

Some persons may listen in a defensive way. Since real listening can be an exhausting experience, they may not be able to receive physically, emotionally, and intellectually and react to all that may be said, so they set up screens to protect themselves. However, this may lead to using those screens to block out what they don't want to hear but perhaps *need* to hear.

A young child whose demands were being ignored by his mother called out in frustration, "Mommy, open up your earlids!"

In church, perhaps we need to open our earlids rather than our eyelids—to *hear* what the speaker is saying rather than to see how he is saying it. As we listen with humility, attentiveness, sincerity, and a desire to learn, an atmosphere of love is created and the power of listening realized.

How shall we listen? King Benjamin said:

My brethren, all ye that have assembled yourselves together, . . . I have not commanded you to come up hither to trifle with the words which I shall speak, but that you should hearken unto me, and open your ears that ye may hear, and your hearts that ye may understand, and your minds that the mysteries of God may be unfolded to your view. (Mosiah 2:9.)

If we are willing to hear and hearken, we will be fed the words of lasting joy and fulfillment. The greatest speaker and teacher who ever lived, Christ himself, said, at the conclusion of one of his sermons, "If any man have ears to hear, let him hear. . . . with what measure ye mete, it shall be measured to you: and unto you that hear shall more be given." (Mark 4:23-24.)

The art of listening is perhaps the most difficult part of the communication process, since there is no direct involvement, no test except self-motivation. Some listeners falsely assume they have no direct responsibility to the speaker as he speaks. Some who come to church primarily serve as bench warmers. The late President J. Golden Kimball of the First Council of the Seventy illustrated this point with this story that may or may not be true, but it certainly illustrates the point. He is reported to have been conducting the concluding business of the quarterly conference of the Juab Stake in central Utah one hot Sunday afternoon. The sustaining of officers by the show of uplifted hands was in process, and he suspected that those in the congregation were mechanically raising hands without thinking or listening. So he droned, "All those in favor of moving Mount Nebo up into the next stake, please signify by the usual sign." The vote was unanimous.

Guide to Good Listening

To help members of the Church receive greater benefit from talks they hear in church, here are some suggested guidelines:

1. Prepare to listen by developing a receptive and optimistic attitude. Try to put into practice in your life words of counsel imparted by each speaker you hear. (See D&C 44:2.)

2. Pray before each meeting for the Spirit to attend the speakers as well as the audience. Pray especially for spiritual gifts of wisdom, knowledge, and understanding. (See D&C 46.)

3. Attend church with a positive attitude and a *desire* to learn.

4. Don't judge speakers by outward appearances. Make allowances for deficiencies in the speaker's delivery, appearance, and character, and focus attention on ideas and content.

5. Hear the speaker out. Don't prematurely reject a subject, or react defensively if you are called to repent or change. Defer your reactions until the end of the speech.

6. Look for personal profit. Find at least one good idea that you can apply in your life personally to build faith and testimony.

7. Work at listening. Good listening takes energy, humility, and a prayerful spirit. Some people daydream because they will not spend the energy to concentrate. Give conscious attention through your posture, eyes, and reactions.

8. Capitalize on "thought speech." The average rate of speaking is about 125 words per minute, while the listener thinks four times that fast. Use this extra time by (a) making mental summaries of what has been said, (b) applying his message to your life, (c) thinking about your knowledge of the subject.

As one begins to listen more effectively, the communication circle is completed from speaker to listener and back. The spoken word from the pulpit needs a listening ear, an open heart, and a contrite spirit. Then "he that preacheth and he that receiveth, understand one another, and both are edified and rejoice together."

CHAPTER 18

When You Ask Others to Speak

The story is told of a college freshman, a convert of only three weeks, who was asked to give his first talk in church. The call came to him as his bishop approached him one Sunday and asked, "Do you think you have enough to say to occupy two or three minutes in sacrament meeting next week? We would like to hear a short testimony."

Nervously, the young man accepted and immediately began experiencing the apprehensions and emotional traumas of a first talk. The following Sunday, after Sunday School, the young man's phone rang. It was the bishop's counselor calling him.

"Our musical number has been cancelled," he began apologetically. "Would you be able to extend your testimony to seven or ten minutes?"

Later, as the perspiring new convert arrived at the chapel, the bishop greeted him at the door with the words, "Brother _____ , our main speaker is sick, so please take as much time as you like. Twenty or thirty minutes would be fine."

This true experience, which occurred nearly twelve years ago, fortunately did not end as disastrously as one might imagine. The young man shared his testimony and conversion story and through divine help was able to occupy the desired time. However, in retelling the story many years later, he admits, "I seriously wondered just what kind of church I had gotten myself into!"

As exceptional as these circumstances were, nonetheless a point might be well taken. What are the responsibilities of those who ask others to speak?

Learning how to be effective in calling others to speak is as vital as learning how to be an effective speaker. Every week throughout the Church, thousands of speakers in sacrament meetings try to motivate people to understand and live gospel truths. Thousands others use the spoken word in Sunday School and other auxiliary meetings, firesides, conferences, priesthood meetings, and funerals. Many of those speeches are effective and uplifting—and some are not. Why? One reason is inadequate prayer and preparation on the part of the person who calls the speaker.

Calling someone to speak is not a trivial or casual assignment, and officers and leaders, youth or adult, must realize their responsibility in ensuring that the pulpit time (which is the Lord's formal teaching time) is used wisely to edify and uplift.

One woman, who had some justified complaints, described her ward situation: "There seems to be no control over the speakers. One evening in sacrament meeting, we had six speakers, members of a family who had just moved into the ward. The wife spoke first about her romance, her children, the dates of their births, on and on, until she had taken up almost the entire time. Then each of her children spoke, followed by her husband. They tried to shorten their talks, but the meeting was running way overtime. The congregation was restless, noisy, and children were crying—and my back was aching. It was *not* a positive experience."

To call speakers who will contribute positively to the meeting, the person who makes the call should develop a certain sensitivity to situations, needs, and individual personalities. He should learn how to effectively train and direct members in fulfilling speaking requests. He should carefully evaluate individuals as prospective speakers. Church members vary in degree of testimony, faith, understanding of gospel principles, and speaking ability. Thus, they vary in their ability to inspire and teach.

Foremost among his responsibilities is to utilize prayer. Helaman tells us to "counsel with the Lord in *all* thy doings." (Alma 37:37. Italics added.) Certainly choosing people to teach the gospel is a worthy task for divine consultation.

Other suggestions for those who ask others to speak include the following:

1. Diagnose the needs of the congregation and situation before prescribing the proper subject matter or speaker. A good Church leader understands and is aware of the hopes, problems, and needs of those for whom he is responsible. He works out of love for them in selecting speakers who will help their spiritual growth.

2. Choose a speaker and topic after prayer and consultation with other Church leaders. Often, consulting with co-workers and other leaders can result in valuable suggestions. Never call a speaker without first seeking spiritual confirmation from the Lord.

3. Ask the speaker far enough in advance to allow for proper preparation, and be specific in your instructions to him.

In asking others to speak, radiate an attitude of love, warmth, confidence, and appreciation. Explain the occasion, the purpose of the talk, the time limits, some of the specific needs of the audience, and, when appropriate, a subject or topic. In general, let him know your expectations of his performance.

A teacher in the Church Educational System was once asked to speak at a sacrament meeting in another stake. He had made careful preparation for the talk. During the sacrament service, the Spirit prompted him as to some needs of the congregation, especially the youth, and he felt inspired to tell two stories that had appropriate humor. Then, just as he got up to speak, the bishop quickly whispered, "I forgot to tell you two things we tell every speaker—we want no dramatics and no humor." As a result, because proper preliminary instruction was not given, some of the effectiveness of the speaker and his message was lost.

4. If no specific topic is assigned, remind the speaker in a positive way of his limitations. Being sensitive to his personality and background, suggest that he avoid topics that are controversial, negative, argumentative, or dealing with mysteries or speculation. Some people have religious "hobby horses" that can be dangerous, since they place too much emphasis on certain ideas and give little heed to others equally important. Occasionally these few will judge and scold fellow members who are not as involved as they are in their particular areas of interest. Sometimes they will even use

speaking opportunities to advertise personal vocational or monetary pursuits.

5. Follow up several days before the meeting with an inquiry about the progress of preparation and to offer help.

6. Have a short meeting with the speaker(s) prior to the meeting at which he is to speak. Review goals, speaking time, and other information pertaining to the meeting. Have vocal prayer, asking for the guidance of the Spirit.

7. Give a brief introduction of the speaker to the congregation, so they will be able to identify with him and become better acquainted with him.

An important part of a successful speech lies not with the speaker but with the leader who has laid the proper groundwork and accomplished the necessary spiritual preparations. As leader and speaker work in harmony, each realizing the importance and responsibility of his assignment, the quality and spirituality of the meeting will be rich and the rewards will be plentiful.

CHAPTER 19

The
Youth Talk

This is an age when many things are termed "mini"—mini-lessons, mini-classes, and even mini-bikes. And even in the Church, the mini-talk, better known as youth speaking, is proving to be a valuable and important part of Church meetings, seminary gatherings, and activity nights. The mini-sermon may range from two-and-one-half-minute talks in Sunday School to five-minute talks in stake conference. Why is youth speaking such a vital part of church? Because some of the most inspiring and spirit-touching talks are given by young people, and because speaking in church is an important growth experience even for the very young.

One bishop commented, "I concentrate much of my interest on the youth of the ward. If you have the youth behind you, you often have the whole ward." He understood the great power of youth, with their zest for life, their endless energy, their desire to achieve.

Wise Church leaders also know that speaking provides valuable ways for youth to grow spiritually and mentally. Speaking, as nerve-wracking as it might seem, helps instill confidence, commitment, and faith, and helps build future missionaries, teachers, businessmen, and church and world leaders.

While many youth talks are motivating and inspiring, there are still some that are not. For example, in one ward a very frank twelve-year-old boy began his talk with this statement: "When my sister or I am asked to give a talk, my dad writes it and my mother corrects it." Then he proceeded to struggle through his talk, and it was obvious that *he* had not prepared it.

Another practice that sometimes emerges in wards is young people merely reading an article or story from a church book or magazine. A "talk" like this is not only boring to the congregation, but it also defeats the purpose of learning to speak. You gain confidence and courage in speaking only as you have success experiences, and those experiences only come through proper preparation.

We might compare giving a talk with taking a trip. When dad announces a family trip, immediately he is bombarded with such questions as: Where are we going? Why are we going? What are we going to do there? What route will we follow? What should we take?

The same questions should arise when you start to plan a speech. You must know your destination, how to get there, what problems you may meet, what materials you will need, and what you will accomplish.

By following the rules of the road, you can arrive at your destination and achieve success more easily and happily. So, let's take a mini-trip to learn six rules leading to a happy and satisfying mini-talk.

First, forget your "hang-ups" and give it a try.

Remember the childhood story of *Snow White and the Seven Dwarfs?* Dopey was the dwarf who couldn't talk. And why could he not talk? Very simple. He had never tried. Don't bow out of a church talk because you are afraid to speak. Be adventuresome!

Second, picture in your mind the destination.

The primary purpose of any church talk is to motivate the listener to be a better church member. Forget about impressing the crowd, but focus intently on wanting to *help* your friends (the audience).

Third, set aside private time to plan your moves.

Choose your subject carefully and prayerfully. In two to five minutes, there is time to discuss only one simple topic, so choose a subject and then list possible topics on which you might focus.

111

Choose a topic that interests you the most, one about which you have convictions, one about which you *want* to talk. Ask for suggestions from family and teachers, but let your speech be the result of your own creative thinking. For ideas, you may wish to refer to one of the Church magazines or a Church book, but use these sources for ideas only. Be original! Decide on your purpose. What do you want to accomplish? How do you want the audience to feel when you finish? What do you want to motivate them to do?

Organize your talk. Since you have time to communicate only one idea, organizing is simple: an introduction, your idea (explained by a scripture and story), and a conclusion.

Fourth, keep within your time limit.

If you are asked to give a two-and-one-half-minute talk, don't mentally change it to three to five minutes. Two minutes is a shorter time than you may think, so plan your moves by practicing timing your talk.

A college girl who was asked to give a short talk in Sunday School prepared and organized diligently. She delivered her talk, and later, a fellow ward member who had been absent from the meeting said to her, "I hear you delivered a *sermon*." As she queried her roommates, she found to her embarrassment that they couldn't remember what she had talked about, only that she talked too long. So stay within the time limit.

Fifth, remember that delivery and appearance are important.

Don't be the one of the following:

—Bashful Beth, who can't look directly at the audience and can't tell you why.

—Stoneface Sam and Rigid Ralph, who never move a muscle.

—Clowning Clem, who tries to be funny but is left waiting for people to laugh.

—Teetering Tammy, who is always off center, her weight slumped on one hip and then the other.

—Leaner Len, who is the picture of acute fatigue as he drapes over the pulpit.

Poise in delivery is not hard to achieve if you use common sense. Don't chew gum, constantly brush your hair back, giggle when you look at your friends, or tell jokes.

Do dress appropriately and modestly, take deep, relaxing

breaths before you stand to speak, look often at encouraging faces as you speak, speak firmly and clearly into the microphone, and smile.

Sixth, never read your talk.

Two methods to use in delivery are (1) to write out the talk and then memorize it, and (2) to use notecards. The memorizing method is sometimes preferred by inexperienced speakers, but if you use this method, take your speech to the pulpit and be very familiar with it so you can look down quickly to find your place if need be. Don't write on both sides of the paper. Use half sheets of paper to make the script less obvious. For the notecard method, simply list main ideas and organization on cards, and write out quotations. Practice your talk at home, in front of a mirror, in your Sunday School class, or with friends. The more practice, the more confident you will feel.

After you have followed these six guidelines, pray earnestly for support and for clarity of voice and mind. Then, as you begin to speak, you will feel the calming influence of the Spirit, and you will be on the road to speaking well.

The following experience illustrates how one youth learned to meet the challenge of speaking in church.

Paul Davis, a priest, was asked by the bishop one Sunday to give a five-minute talk in sacrament meeting the following Sunday. He didn't know what to talk about when he was asked, and he was very upset. He didn't dare say no since he felt, especially since he was a holder of the priesthood, that it was his duty to act for God.

When Paul arrived home, he told his father that he had been asked to talk in church and that he was afraid to talk before so many people. Paul's father smiled at him and said, "I know it is difficult to give a talk sometimes. You are probably concerned about what to say, aren't you." Then he sat down with Paul and talked the matter over with him. He pointed out to Paul that he should talk about something in which he had a personal interest, such as prayer. "Since you only have five minutes you can't cover very much." he said, "but why don't you tell the members how God answers prayers. Remember how your prayers were answered when you were recovering from your automobile accident?"

113

When the time came to give the talk, Paul was more excited than scared. After the sacrament meeting the bishop said to him: "Paul, that was really an inspiring talk. You sounded as if you meant every word." Paul replied, "Yes, it makes a difference when you talk about something you are interested in and know something about."

Each young person can achieve and enjoy Paul's type of success, but each one must pay the price that Paul paid—think, pray, prepare, and practice.

In planning and preparing your talk, you may find it helpful to use the following outline. How the outline works is given in a sample talk titled "God Answers Prayers."

Sample Outline

   I. Introduction
      A.   Capture attention with a story, scripture, quotation
      B.   Begin stating your idea immediately. Don't tell the whys and whens of being asked to speak. Don't apologize for anything. Memorize your introduction.
  II. Body
      A.   Explain your main idea by using:
          1. Example
          2. Story or personal experience
          3. Scripture
 III. Conclusion
      A.   Repeat the main idea, giving a challenge or suggestion for applying the idea.
      B.   Close with the words "In the name of Jesus Christ. Amen." (Don't say, "In the name of *thy* Son." This is used only in addressing the Father in prayer.)

God Answers Prayers

Quotation: "Who rises from prayer a better man, his prayer is answered," stated the British poet George Meredith.

Example: Jerry was afraid of the dark. One night as he lay in bed, frightened by every noise, real or imagined, he decided to pray that his fear would leave him. Somehow he found enough courage to climb out of his

114

Scripture: bed and kneel by it. After his prayer he felt peace and calm, and soon fell asleep.

Scripture: "And all things whatsoever ye shall ask in prayer, believing, ye shall receive." (Matthew 21:22.)

Example: The Lord does hear and answer prayers, as shown in thousands of testimonies. He may answer yes, or no, or wait—and wait is probably the most frequent answer. Here is an example: President David O. McKay tells of a time during his youth when he was in the mountains looking for stray cattle. As he stopped to give his horse a rest, he had an intense desire to have a manifestation that the restored gospel was true. He got off his horse, knelt under a serviceberry bush, and prayed, but nothing happened. Years later this prayer was answered, when the spiritual manifestation he had prayed for as a boy came as a natural result of his missionary labors.

Story: Your personal experience or an experience of a member of your immediate family or an ancestor.

Concluding
Quotation: The late Elder Matthew Cowley of the Council of the Twelve said, "God does not always answer our prayers the way we want them answered, but if the channel is open, I testify to you that he answers them the way they should be answered, and those answers are for our best good and have an eternal and lasting value." (*Matthew Cowley Speaks* [Deseret Book, 1954], p. 21.)

Checklist for Youth Speakers

_____ 1. Have I made proper mental and spiritual preparation? Have I written down what I already know about my topic?

_____ 2. Have I selected my subject carefully, organized one good point, and supported it with examples, stories, a scripture, or a quotation?

_____ 3. Is my speech basically the result of my own efforts (with some help from parents or teachers)?

_____ 4. Have I avoided humor that would distract from my message or the spirituality of the meeting?

_____ 5. Have I made an outline of my talk?

_____ 6. Have I practiced my talk sufficiently so I do not have to read it?

_____ 7. Am I aware of the importance of good posture, dress, manners, language?

CHAPTER 20

The Impromptu Talk

The congregation had just settled back to enjoy the sacrament meeting sermons when the bishop stepped to the pulpit. "Today, we have a very special meeting planned on the theme 'A Latter-day Saint in Today's World.' We do not have assigned speakers because we want to hear from you. Will the following people come to the stand and share with us a five-minute talk on that subject: Brother Anderson, Sister Palmer . . ."

This situation is not uncommon to church members, yet it may be accompanied with near heart failure, when you hear your own name called from the pulpit.

Someone once said, "You can tell the kind of wheels a man has in his head by the spokes that come out of his mouth." That is perhaps the silent fear common to impromptu speakers. As much as you might wish you had stayed home, you can't help but feel a pleasurable glow when you have given an impromptu talk successfully. Yet, it *is* a challenging situation.

How can you meet this situation more confidently?

Remember that much of our conversation is nothing more than a series of impromptu talks, speech that we have not had opportunity to prepare beforehand, such as in testimony meeting. One of the real values of this type of talk is that it is fresh, spontaneous, and sincere. In the impromptu talk, personal experiences are usually used more often than in a formal, previously assigned talk, and so the talk becomes more personal.

Use the few moments between the call to speak and your first words to bring your emotions under control and plan what you will say. Say a silent prayer and ask for divine guidance and strength. Then listen for the promptings of the Spirit. Do not waste emotional energy with feelings of fear or despair. Recognize that a rush of adrenalin into the bloodstream is inevitable, for this is nature's way of preparing the body for an emergency. Be grateful that you are so stimulated; without such motivational power you probably would not meet the occasion adequately. However, this surge of energy does need to be controlled.

Relax by taking several deep breaths. Then rise calmly and walk to the podium deliberately and without hesitation nor undue haste. Look squarely at the audience, take a full breath, and start to speak.

Even though you may be speaking without much advance warning, almost any impromptu speech can be organized to a certain extent. When you are called, mentally ask yourself three questions:

1. What do I want to motivate the audience to do?
2. What general truth can I present about the subject?
3. What personal experience can I relate about the subject?

When you deliver the talk, *reverse* the order;

1. Relate a personal experience to illustrate your subject.
2. Point out the general truth as suggested by your personal story.
3. Tie the story and truth together in a statement asking for action, and bear your testimony of this subject.

Here are some general guidelines for impromptu speaking:

1. Ask for and respond to the promptings of the Spirit.
2. Begin your talk immediately, and don't discuss how difficult it is to give it. Never apologize.
3. Don't hesitate to relate the topic to personal experience. It is easier to speak about something you know.
4. If your mind goes blank as you are speaking, summarize what you have just said. This allows you to go back and retrace your thoughts, then pick up again.

5. Be brief. The less you speak, the less chance there is that your talk will become jumbled.

6. Don't try to be clever by telling jokes. Your responsibility is to inspire, not entertain.

7. Look confident, be specific, and be positive.

8. Quit while you are ahead. Too often, a person will give a good impromptu speech but then, because his momentary success has given him a feeling of confidence, he will ramble on and destroy whatever communication he might have had.

9. End on a positive note.

Types of Preparation

Wise Latter-day Saints will prepare for impromptu speaking opportunities. One leader prepared a talk each week, pretending he was to give a talk in church. He prepared many talks that were never given, but one Sunday he was called from the audience to speak, and he was prepared.

A mission president told his missionaries that in every meeting they attended, they should mentally prepare a talk based on the words of the opening hymn, and then, if they were ever called on to speak and could think of nothing else, they could use that as their text. Another person keeps in his wallet a list of topics and examples that he can use at any time. One topic is listed as "Horse and Neglect," to remind him of a talk topic on neglect, with a story about a horse to illustrate.

Story: *Once there was a horse that ran away early in the morning and didn't return home until late at night. His master greeted him with bitter words of condemnation. In response, the horse replied, "But here I am safe and sound. You have your horse." "True," replied the master, "but my field is unplowed."*

If a man turns to God in his old age or in his spare time, God may finally get the man, but he has been defrauded of the man's work. And the man himself has been defrauded most of all.

Conclusion: *The story can also be tied to the parable of the talents to clinch the point of "the penalties of neglect" in the conclusion.*

This person recommends making a list of items, topics, or

stories, quotations, and scriptures with which one is familiar, and keeping the list in one's wallet or purse.

President David O. McKay committed many poems to memory, which was a fruitful source for talks from which he could draw throughout his life.

Family home evening is an excellent time to train family members to speak on a moment's notice. If it is not overdone, it can become an exciting learning experience for all.

One time a friend asked a church leader how he had gained so much gospel knowledge. The leader replied that when he was driving along in his car he would say out loud, "Our next speaker will now be Brother _____, who will give us a five-minute talk on _____." (And he would say whatever topic popped into his head.) Then he would drive along pretending he was in church, and he would deliver his talk aloud. He said this helped him tremendously in speaking.

As traumatic as impromptu speaking may seem, it is a valuable means of inspiring others and growing personally. As you increase your knowledge of the gospel and your spiritual experience, you will have more resource material from which to draw. And, as you fearlessly bear your testimony and mentally prepare for impromptu speaking situations, you will grow more confident in speaking.

Following is an impromptu speech given by a young man in sacrament meeting.

Impromptu Speech

SUBJECT; What it means to be a Latter-day Saint in today's world
TOPIC: "Love at Home"
One of my favorite hymns is the one we sang as our opening hymn tonight. To me it is the essence of what it means to be a Latter-day Saint in today's world.

Kindly heaven smiles above
When there's love at home;
All the world is filled with love
When there's love at home. . . .
Oh, there's One who smiles on high
When there's love at home.

I remember as a young boy being very sick with a high fever and needing constant care. My father gave me a blessing and my mother sat by my bed day and night with very little sleep until I was better. That experience left a great impression on me. I knew my parents loved me.

What does it mean to be a Latter-day Saint in today's world? It means that in a world full of broken homes and lack of love, there is still beauty to be found and shared if there's love at home. As Latter-day Saints, we are taught the importance of having love and joy in our homes. This is the challenge for church members in today's world—to add beauty to the world by creating love at home.

My father was a bishop when I was a teenager, and even though he was busy, he still took time to take me to movies and ball games and on outings. When there is love such as this in the home, the problems of the world seem to fade away. Children grow up secure and happy. They have an inner strength from knowing their parents love them unconditionally.

Now that I am a parent myself, love at home has an even greater meaning to me. When my little daughter says, "I love you, Daddy," my fatigue and problems disappear and the world is beautiful.

Time doth softly, sweetly glide
When there's love at home.

We as Latter-day Saints have a responsibility to ourselves, to our families, and to our Father in heaven to see that our homes are filled with love and contentment. This wonderful gospel principle has brought great joy to me, and I pray it will bring great joy to all of us as we recommit ourselves to making the world a better place by having love at home.

CHAPTER 21

The
Fireside Talk

In pioneer times, after the evening meal was over and the children had been put to bed, the dinner guests would often gather around the fireside. There, as the fire popped and crackled, they would spend the evening discussing the gospel, exchanging stories, and sharing experiences. It was a favorite time in those days of rigorous frontier life.

Today, just as in former times, fireside meetings are a popular way to share the gospel. Even the basic purposes of firesides have not changed: to learn gospel principles through faith-promoting and informal teaching, to provide opportunities to discuss problems and bear testimony, and to provide fellowship among special age and interest groups.

A fireside speaker has a special opportunity, since his listeners have chosen to be at this extra meeting. He can have a powerful inflence on lives if he imparts knowledge in an appropriate and effective way. For some young people, information gleaned from firesides deeply influences their desires and goals. Often they feel more free to discuss their problems and concerns and to ask pertinent questions concerning the gospel.

Preparing the Talk

When you are asked to speak in a fireside gathering, find out as much as you can about the group involved—their age level, interests, concerns, needs, and desires. Be sure you understand the nature of the meeting, whether it is to be a large gathering where a more formal approach would be more effective, or a small, intimate group that meets in a home setting or Relief Society room. Sometimes a subject is preassigned; often a person is asked to speak because of his knowledge or experiences in a particular area of interest. However, you may be asked to select your own subject and approach. If so, here are some general guidelines to help you.

1. Remember the purposes of your presentation—to inform, convert, inspire, comfort, challenge, guide. Decide what you want to accomplish, and then go to the scriptures and other sources for help.

2. Select material that can be used with new, different, and creative approaches.

3. Be sure the subject you select is suitable for the age group and interests of the audience. Do not talk down to them.

4. Avoid topics that are controversial, argumentative, or deal with speculation.

5. Use humor wisely and sparingly. A fireside talk should primarily inspire, not entertain.

6. Know your subject well enough that you can look directly at your audience. Be personable and enthusiastic.

Conducting a Discussion

Some of the most successful firesides are those in which the group participates in a discussion, under the leadership of the speaker. Not every speaker feels comfortable with this approach, but with practice, you can become a better discussion leader—and the benefits inherent in the group's participation are well worth considering this type of approach. Here are some suggestions to help you become a better discussion leader, whether in a classroom or in a fireside.

1. Plan the discussion questions ahead of time, but do not structure them so rigidly that you cannot listen to the concerns and interests of your audience. Sometimes their responses will indicate a different direction should be taken in the discussion.

2. Establish some ground rules for the discussion, either expressed verbally to the group or established in your own mind. You must maintain control of the situation at all times.

123

3. Try to keep the responses brief and to the point.

4. Draw responses from as many persons as possible, and avoid allowing one or two persons to dominate the discussion.

5. Keep the discussion on the subject. If it does drift away, tactfully bring it back to the point you wish to make. (Sometimes, however, you may take your cues from the group and use the discussion to help you determine the direction to take. The key word is flexibility.)

6. Do not allow the discussion to become a conversation or dialogue between individuals. Be sure the entire group is involved.

7. At the conclusion of the discussion, summarize the points that have been made.

Using Audiovisual Aids

Fireside messages can often be greatly enhanced through the use of audiovisual materials. However, they should be planned well and should be appropriate to your subject and method of presentation. They should supplement the message, not be a substitute for it. Among materials that may be used effectively are chalkboards, films, slides, maps, charts, and recordings. Preview your materials beforehand to be sure they fit in with the message.

Give some introductory remarks before using the audiovisual aids, and suggest some things the group might be looking for as you make your presentation.

As you speak, direct your voice and eyes to the audience; don't talk to a map or chalkboard. Passing out papers or other exhibits during the talk can also distract your listeners.

After using any audiovisual materials, discuss the learning experience with the group in relation to the subject, and encourage audience feedback.

As you become more experienced at fireside speaking, you will find yourself relaxing and enjoying the meeting yourself, thus adding to the relaxed atmosphere of the fireside. However, remember that even though a fireside is generally an informal meeting, you must not become too informal in your approach. Always keep in mind that the meeting is designed to uplift, feed spiritually, and change lives for the better.

124

As you take these suggestions to heart and work at improving your speaking skills, perhaps you will one day hear feedback such as the comment of one teenager: "I appreciate fireside talks because they really help me with my problems and help me set goals and pattern my life for the future."

Outline for a Fireside Talk
"Why Temple Marriage"
  I. Introduction
     A. The story of "Little Joe," as told by President Harold B. Lee (see story following outline).
     B. Ask: Why is the temple so special?
 II. Body of Talk
     A. A marriage within the temple is a marriage within the covenant.
        1. It is not the building itself that makes a temple marriage, but the covenants of marriage.
        2. What are these covenants? Discuss history of covenants, from Abraham to Isaac (Genesis 24) to present time.
     B. Why are we a covenant people today?
        1. We are a "holy people," chosen because God loves us and because he will keep his oath to Abraham and his seed. (Deuteronomy 7:2-3, 6-9.)
        2. We are a peculiar people. Explain.
     C. Reasons for setting marriage in the temple as a goal.
        1. Statistics on divorces between those married in the temple and those married by civil authority.
        2. Marriage for eternity is marriage performed in God's way.
        3. Children of a temple marriage are born under the covenant.
        4. Testimonial of a couple who have been married in the temple.
     D. How to prepare to qualify for temple marriage.
        1. Discussion or testimonial on dating.
        2. Bishop's interview.
III. Conclusion
     A. Sealing the covenants in love.

1. Are we in the temple, or is the temple in us?
2. We have a lifetime to seal the promise.

B. Challenge to begin now to be worthy of these covenants.
C. Share this knowledge and testimony with others not present at fireside.
D. Bear testimony of temple marriage.

"Little Joe"

President Harold B. Lee, at general conference in April 1957, said, ". . . I would like to speak briefly about the sacred ordinance of temple marriage which is so vital to every human soul." He then told this true story as related by a temple watchman.

"One morning not so long ago I was sitting at the desk in the temple gate house reading when my attention was drawn to a knock on the door. There stood two little boys, ages about seven or eight years. As I opened the door, I noticed that they were poorly dressed and had been neither washed nor combed. They appeared as if they had left home before Father or Mother had awakened that morning. As I looked beyond these little fellows, I saw two infants in pushcarts. In answer to my question as to what they wanted, one of the boys pointed to his little brother in the cart and replied: 'His name is Joe. Will you shake hands with little Joe? It is little Joe's birthday—he is two years old today, and I want him to touch the temple so when he gets to be an old man he will remember he touched the temple when he was two years old.'

"Pointing to the other little boy in the other cart, he said this: 'This is Mark, he's two years old, too.' Then, with a solemn, reverent attitude rare in children so young, he asked: 'Now can we go over there and touch the temple?' I replied: 'Sure you can.' They pushed their little carts over to the temple and lifted the infants up, and placed their hands against that holy building. Then as I stood there with a lump in my throat, I heard the little boy say to his infant brother, 'Now, Joe, you will always remember when you was two years old you touched the temple.' They thanked me and departed for home." (*Conference Report*, April 1957, pp. 20-21.)

CHAPTER 22

Speaking in Sacrament Meeting

One of the greatest challenges for the church speaker is that of speaking in sacrament meeting, for the purpose of this meeting, the Lord has told us, is "to pay thy devotions unto the Most High." (D&C 59:10.)

At this important meeting, members partake of the sacrament, one of the most sacred ordinances of the Church, signifying their remembrance of the Savior and his atoning sacrifice. Then they are in a reverent spirit of worship, ready to hear words of inspiration and faith. President Joseph Fielding Smith said he knew of no other place "where we can gather where we should be more reflective and solemn and where more of the spirit of worship should be maintained."

What kind of talk should one give to be in keeping with the spirit of the sacrament?

In answer to that question, remember first the purposes of gospel instruction: to present specific gospel principles in an understandable way, and to give encouragement, renew faith, and strengthen determination.

If no topic is suggested, choose a specific one and check with a member of the bishopric to be sure it will be in keeping with the spirit of the meeting and that no one else on the program will be speaking on the same topic.

Mental and spiritual preparation are essential for effective gospel speaking, so avoid Saturday night and Sunday afternoon preparation. Select your topic far enough in advance so you can prepare well and thoughtfully.

Take time to pray about your talk, and seek divine confirmation and assurance.

Select a message that will be understood as much as possible by all ages in the congregation.

Use scriptures in your talk, but select short verses that support the topic, not lengthy passages that must be read. Stick to Church doctrine and authoritative sources, and avoid controversial or speculative statements.

Be positive in your approach, using interesting, appealing stories and avoiding scolding or preaching, as exemplified in such verbs as *ought, should,* and *don't.*

Remember also that sacrament meeting is not a place to deliver a travelogue.

As you deliver the talk, try to have the content well in mind so you can use a conversational approach, reading only scriptures and other quotations. (Rehearse quotations, if necessary, so you can read them smoothly and well.) Speak with enthusiasm and conviction.

And last—and most important—stop on time. Do not use time that has been assigned to other speakers. It's better to stop early than late!

Outline of a Sacrament Meeting Talk

"Faith in Action"

I. Introduction
   A. Personal story of how faith was tested as a teenager
   B. Lesson on faith from life of Porter Rockwell

II. Body of the talk
   A. Definitions of faith
      1. ". . . things hoped for"—Hebrews 11:1
      2. ". . . first great governing principle"—Joseph Smith
   B. Power of active faith
      1. Examples from biblical days
      2. Examples from today
         a. President Spencer W. Kimball

   b. Young mother-to-be
   c. Prisoner of war in Viet Nam
   d. Personal examples from own life
  C. Developing and increasing faith
   1. Two steps to nourishing seed of faith
    a. Studying the gospel to learn of and increase faith in Jesus Christ
    b. Keeping the commandments
     (1) Example of Joseph in Egypt
     (2) Joseph Smith praying in the woods
  D. Evaluating our level of faith
   1. Examining our works
   2. Questions for self-analysis
III. Conclusion
  A. Appeal to audience to follow steps of increasing faith
  B. Appeal to audience to turn passive belief into active faith

CHAPTER 23

Bearing Your Testimony

The scene is a testimony meeting. From the congregation rises a teenage boy who is preparing for a mission. He expresses his appreciation for church standards and the blessings he receives from living them. He expresses admiration for his priesthood adviser, his seminary teacher, his family.

Then from the far side of the chapel an older woman slowly rises. In firm, clear tones, she speaks of her conviction of gospel principles and relates a heartwarming story of an unusual healing that came as an answer to fasting and prayer.

An eight-year-old girl quickly stands and shares her happiness that she is to be baptized. She is thrilled that her father will be able to baptize her, and she tearfully thanks her family and friends for their love.

So goes the testimony meeting, as members from all walks of life stand to bear their testimonies. There is a warm feeling in the room, and those present know that they will leave the meeting feeling uplifted and inspired by the Spirit.

President David O. McKay said, "Inspiration, revelation to the individual soul is the rock upon which a testimony should be built and there is not one living who cannot get it if he will conform to those laws and live a clean life which will permit the Holy Spirit to place that testimony in him." (Church Section of the *Deseret News*, September 12, 1951, p. 4.)

Joy and peace come through a testimony of the gospel of Jesus Christ. Exposure to and even knowledge of Christian principles are not enough. It is the testimony, the affirmation, that one receives of eternal truths that motivates him to change his life for the better.

An important part of the perfection process is the practice among Latter-day Saints of sharing their testimonies with one another, thereby receiving strength, hope, and comfort. Church members have the privilege of attending testimony meetings frequently, and each person is expected to come with a prayerful and humble spirit. These meetings can be wonderful spiritual feasts if each one has made the proper preparations and has the right attitude toward the testimonial.

To testify is to bear witness. When an individual testifies, he bears witness to the truthfulness of something he has experienced through the physical senses, through reason, or through spiritual enlightenment. A personal testimony comes from personal knowledge or experience and is given with the most solemn intent to others. Although one can share his testimony with others, each person should also develop this assurance for himself.

What truths should be expressed and declared in a testimony of the gospel? In the Doctrine and Covenants we read:

For all have not every gift given unto them; for there are many gifts, and to every man is given a gift by the Spirit of God.

To some is given one, and to some is given another, that all may be profited thereby.

To some it is given by the Holy Ghost to know that Jesus Christ is the Son of God, and that he was crucified for the sins of the world.

To others it is given to believe on their words, that they also might have eternal life if they continue faithful. (D&C 46:11-14.)

Thus we see that a testimony should include knowledge that Jesus Christ is the Son of God and Savior of the world. It should also include witness that Joseph Smith is the prophet of God through whom the gospel was restored in the latter days. A third component of a testimony is knowledge that The Church of Jesus Christ of Latter-day Saints is "the only true and living church upon the face of the whole earth. . . ." (D&C 1:30.)

131

How does one obtain a testimony? President Joseph Fielding Smith declared:

A testimony may come through the senses of hearing, seeing, or feeling. In relation to the gospel, a testimony is a revelation to the individual who earnestly seeks one by prayer, study, and faith. It is the impression or speaking of the Holy Ghost to the soul in a convincing, positive manner. It is something which is far more penetrating than impressions from any other source, but it cannot fully be described. (Answers to Gospel Questions, *vol. III* [Deseret Book, *1960*], *p. 28.*)

Latter-day Saints—members of the true church of Christ—testify that the gospel is true and voice the joy they find in this knowledge. A testimony of this truth comes from desire, study, prayer, practice, service, and obedience to the commandments.

When you feel inspired to bear your testimony, here are some do's and don'ts you might consider:

1. Do speak because you feel you have something to say, not because you feel that you should say something. If you do not feel that your testimony is strong, you can express gratitude to God for the many blessings you enjoy.

2. Do remember that a testimony should be spontaneous, from the heart, and prompted by the Spirit. Do not worry about eloquent phrasing. It should not be a formal speech that is composed prior to the meeting or from notes written down during the meeting. However, you may wish to organize your thoughts.

3. Don't feel obligated to speak just because there is a silence between testimonies. Oftentimes this silence can provide a period of worthwhile, thoughtful meditation.

4. Do speak loud enough so everyone can hear you. If a microphone is used, speak directly into it, but do not get so close that your words will be distorted by the sound.

5. Do be positive in your remarks. Avoid being critical of yourself by discussing your faults and sins, of being critical of others and their beliefs, or of setting yourself up as being superior, with statements such as "You should," "Do this," etc.

6. Don't moralize or philosophize in your remarks.

7. Don't discuss family affairs or personal troubles unless they

illustrate how one can overcome or solve a problem that would be motivating and inspiring to others. People have enough problems of their own.

8. Do exercise caution in using personal experiences of faith. There is danger in revealing intimate details and discussing in public sacred experiences, such as your patriarchal blessing.

9. Don't use time for bearing testimonies as a time for discussing your pet subjects unless they pertain to your own testimony. This is not a time to deliver a sermon on the welfare plan, genealogy, or any other gospel program or principle except as it pertains directly to your testimony.

10. Do be brief in your remarks.

11. Don't give a travelogue.

12. Do be sincere, humble, and truthful in your remarks. Don't bear testimony of things you don't believe or understand.

13. Don't be reluctant to bear your testimony because you feel inferior to others. The magnitude of a testimony is not significant; what *is* important is the attitude and spirit with which you speak.

Children can be taught early to bear their testimonies. They can learn to recognize the blessings they enjoy and to express appreciation for these blessings. Then, as they learn more about the gospel, "line upon line, precept upon precept," their confidence will become stronger.

Some people hesitate to bear testimony for fear of becoming overly emotional. The Prophet Joseph Smith explained that often in a spiritual setting, tears are a sign of the Holy Ghost. The beauty of testimony bearing lies in the very fact that people share those feelings dearest to them. With testimony bearing comes great spiritual strength.

The primary benefit of bearing your testimony is the blessing that comes to you. Just as you are strengthened from hearing the witness of others, so you also are strengthened by bearing aloud your own personal testimony. As you draw upon your personal experiences and organize your testimony to share it with others, you will be able to see your own feelings more clearly.

The light of Christ that is within all men is sometimes called *conscience*, and it is this conscience, or spirit, that motivates them to seek and gain a testimony. It is this spirit that whispers, "What can I do to get closer to the Savior?" It is this spirit that gives one feelings deep within of wanting to improve, to be more aware of faults that must be forsaken, of sins that must be repented of, of virtues that must be developed.

As you listen to your conscience and determine to obey the commandments of God, you'll find your ability and confidence expanding, and your faith, conviction, and testimony being strengthened.

A beautiful example of testimony bearing is found in the testimony of Elder Melvin J. Ballard of the Council of the Twelve:

. . . I know, within my heart and soul, as I live, that Jesus Christ is the Son of God, the Savior of the world. When I shall stand before Him, in His presence and see Him face to face as He is, I shall not know any better the truth that He is the Christ, and that He lives, than I do today by the witness and testimony of the Spirit of God in my heart and soul. By that same power I know that this is God's work; that Joseph Smith is His prophet, and that the leaders of this Church today enjoy the revelation and the inspiration of God . . . (*Forace Green,* Testimonies of Our Leaders [*Bookcraft, 1958*], *p. 172.*)

This is the testimony for which millions of people in the world today are searching. How eager each of us should be to share it!

CHAPTER 24

The
Funeral Sermon

The purpose of funeral sermons is three-fold: First, to pay worthy tribute to one who has lived a useful life; second, to give comfort to bereaved loved ones; third to awaken a desire and a faith in the hearts of those who listen to serve God and to keep His commandments. (Church News, *October 14, 1961, p. 8.)*

This statement by President David O. McKay expresses the special challenge of funeral speakers.

The Lord has said, "Thou shalt live together in love, insomuch that thou shalt weep for the loss of them that die. . . ." (D&C 42:45.) A funeral is an emotional experience for the loved ones of a person who dies, and they are, therefore, to listen to and hear words of comfort and peace. Kind words and other expressions of sympathy help lift their burden.

If you are asked to speak at a funeral, your obligation is to bring hope and courage to the bereaved. It is a time for humility, compassion, and empathy, not a time to deliver a lengthy sermon.

The Savior taught many remarkable lessons of compassion; during the Sermon on the Mount, he said, "Blessed are they that mourn: for they shall be comforted." (Matthew 5:4.) A most revealing act of compassion occurred as he came to the home of Martha and Mary and found them weeping for their brother Lazarus, who had died. Jesus had told Martha that her brother "shall rise again."

Martha remarked that she knew "that he shall rise again in the resurrection at the last day." Then Jesus said to her, "I am the resurrection, and the life: he that believeth in me, though he were dead, yet shall he live; and whosoever liveth and believeth in me shall never die. . . ." (See John 11:17-26.)

This is the kind of love and the faith you must give to your listeners. As you prepare, be prayerful and ask yourself a few basic questions:

1. How well do I know the deceased?
2. Who can give me greater insight into his life and accomplishments?
3. What are the needs now of the loved ones?
4. What inspiring gospel message will help them the most?

Generally, a funeral will have more than one speaker, and when this is the case, the following approach may be helpful: (1) The first speaker may discuss the personal and family life of the deceased, the eulogy, and (2) the second speaker may present a gospel message. This does not, of course, exclude other speakers from presenting their own personal feelings about the individual.

The Eulogy

The word *eulogy* means good word. It is very proper to speak a good word about the deceased, especially if the message can be turned to a practical application to living, to inspire the listener to incorporate worthy virtues in his life.

The eulogy should praise and evaluate the individual favorably, emphasizing his finer qualities and characteristics and the good he accomplished. Mention his contributions to society, the community, the church, and his friends and family. You might:

1. Point out the struggles he made to achieve his aims.
2. Show the development of his ideas and ideals.
3. Describe his relations and services to his family and fellowmen and indicate their significance.
4. Relate the purpose of life and the blessings of the gospel.
5. Stress how the gospel influenced the life of the deceased.

In building your speech chronologically or topically, do not compile a simple biographical sketch. If you do, you will have an informative speech but not a eulogy. Rather, tell how the deceased

136

reacted to events in his life and what happened as a result of them, excluding unimportant details. For example, if you were eulogizing a person who had suffered with a lengthy illness in life, you would want to show how his illness became a challenge to him and how he resolved to live a good life despite this problem.

Essential to a funeral speech is finding the good. Regardless of how a person has lived according to the speaker's standards, there is always something of worth that can be found. Be careful never to say anything that might be construed as criticism. Do not apologize for the person, but show that despite shortcomings, he was good.

A certain man who died was regarded as a community vagrant. The bishop approached another man who was in the habit of speaking words of praise about every person he knew and said, "Now here is a person about whom you cannot find any good thing to say." The man replied, "He was the best whistler I ever knew. He cheered me up many times with his whistling."

While there is good in every individual, use caution in erasing faults. Praising or glorifying to excess the virtues of faithless persons may create the appearance that living gospel standards in this life is not really important. Make promises about eternal life only if you are inspired strongly by the Spirit. Be careful also to stay within your time limit.

If you are the only speaker, eulogizing the individual should not be the content of your whole speech. Time must be allowed for discussing some type of gospel theme. People often listen more attentively to a funeral sermon than to most speeches. The funeral sermon is not a time for preachment for conversion nor a time to harass the audience, but it is a time to offer guidance, encouragement, and inspiration to those in the audience.

One church leader who has spoken at many funerals explains his approach in delivering a eulogy: "My own formula is to first find out all I can about the deceased, for you can always find admirable qualities. I select three or four of the principal qualities and then work in gospel beliefs to show how important the qualities are. In so doing, I pay him tribute. He may have had Word of Wisdom problems, for example, but if he was faithful to his wife and family, I discuss how important this is and how such devotion can be perpetuated for the eternities."

Here is an opportunity to explain man's purpose on earth and what he must do to be saved. There are usually in attendance persons who are nonmembers and others who seldom attend church. These factors need to be considered. Again, your message should carry a feeling of warmth, tenderness, sympathy, and assurance.

In the funeral eulogy is where you have the opportunity to teach that Jesus is the resurrection and the life. We may not see our loved ones restored immediately to life as Lazarus was brought back from the dead, but we do believe that Jesus has power to bring forth our loved ones from the grave.

Isaiah had faith in the resurrection many centuries before Jesus walked among men, for he said, "He will swallow up death in victory; and the Lord God will wipe away tears from off all faces. . . ." (Isaiah 25:8.)

John the Revelator said, "And I heard a great voice out of heaven saying, Behold, the tabernacle of God is with men, and he will dwell with them, and they shall be his people, and God himself shall be with them, and be their God. And God shall wipe away all tears from their eyes; and there shall be no more death, neither sorrow, nor crying, neither shall there be any more pain: for the former things are passed away." (Revelation 21:3-4.)

Gospel Message

The second type of funeral speech, the gospel message, usually centers upon a gospel theme rather than the life of the deceased. Perhaps the greatest danger of the gospel message talk is when the speaker gives his "pet talk" on his favorite gospel subject. A funeral service is not the place for this type of talk, and great care should be taken to avoid preaching or giving a favorite church sermon unless it relates to the deceased or the purpose of life and the resurrection.

One person tells about how he has always resented the "eloquent church orator" who spoke at his grandmother's funeral and gave a talk on the Book of Mormon, with no reference to the deceased.

Careful organization of speech materials is important in the funeral sermon, to assure coherence of thought and brevity of expression. Poetry quoted should be of fine quality, and spiritual passages quoted should be short and integral to the sermon.

Material for a funeral sermon may be found in biographies, newspapers, magazines, scriptures, books, genealogical records, poetry, and similar sources, but all material should be used with discretion.

One of the great challenges of both the eulogy and the gospel message sermon is getting started. One good approach is to start with a scripture, such as 1 Corinthians 2:9, John 3:16, or Psalm 23.

In delivering the funeral sermon or eulogy, observe all the requirements of good speech delivery. Just as you should never apologize for the life of the deceased, you should also never apologize for being asked to speak. Do not call attention to yourself rather than your remarks.

Deliver the sermon in the very best language. This is not an opportunity to make an impression on strangers or friends with high-powered oratory, but neither should you restrain your voice and speak so softly that it's difficult to hear you; use a normal speaking voice. As you deliver your sermon, you may feel some emotion, but do not be embarrassed. Your emotions can be a source of power.

In preparing your funeral gospel message, secure adequate and factual information, eliminating material that might cause people to become overly upset or embarrassed.

In selecting your material, look for the answers to these questions: Where did we come from? Why are we here? Where are we going? Discuss the plan of salvation, the purpose of earth life, the reality of the resurrection, the assurance of immortality for all, and the hope of eternal life for the faithful.

Remind the family that the deceased has fulfilled his purposes of mortality and has gone to a more beautiful world, where he is free from sadness and pain. Despite death, life goes on, and the deceased would want the family to meet death bravely and love one another all the more out of tribute to him.

Special care must be taken at a funeral for one who has taken his own life. The most appropriate course at such services is probably to deliver a gospel message. Persons may or may not be

139

accountable for their actions, and persons under great stress may lose the ability to reason to the point that they would no longer be accountable for their acts. However, all judgment must be reserved for the Lord, not for a funeral speaker.

At any funeral service, regardless of the circumstances, emotions are under great stress, and you as speaker should be considerate. Your message should be just long enough to pay tribute to the deceased, long enough to give words of comfort to the bereaved, long enough to instill added faith, reassurance, and consolation by means of the gospel of Jesus Christ.

If you are sincere, well-prepared, and aware of your great responsibility, you will be able to pay tribute, give comfort, edify, and instill faith, and the listener will leave the service with gratitude for the gospel of Jesus Christ, inspired and motivated to put his life in order, to be a better person, and to prepare to someday meet his Maker.

Sample Outline for a Funeral Eulogy

I. Positive influences of the life of the deceased
   A. Reflections and comments from those associated with him in:
      1. Family life
      2. Church activity
      3. Professional and occupational pursuits
      4. Neighborhood and civic work

II. Admirable qualities and accomplishments (Substitute actual qualities for these examples)
   A. Industrious
   B. Honest, truthful, full of integrity, and reliability
   C. Loved life, loved the Lord, and loved his fellowmen
   D. Faithful in keeping covenants and in service to God and others

III. Application of these qualities to life
   A. How they relate to the gospel
   B. What they mean to us, the living
   C. How we can live to honor the deceased and God

Sample Outline for a Gospel Message Sermon

   I. Purpose of life
      A. To achieve immortality and eternal life: examples of some of the Christ-like qualities of the deceased
      B. A time for trial and testing: examples of trials the deceased had to bear
      C. A time for men to prepare to meet God: examples of how the deceased was prepared
  II. The reality of the resurrection
      A. Christ's gift to all mankind
      B. A time of reunion with our loved ones
 III. Trust in God
      A. No one needs to bear the sorrow of death alone
      B. Heavenly Father helps us to go on living courageously, with inner peace, and with the assurance of eternal reunion
 IV. Putting our own lives in order
      A. We will be judged for our works on earth
      B. Righteous living is the greatest earthly tribute to the deceased

Suggested Scriptures for a Funeral Sermon

The following scriptures deal with the resurrection and the purpose of life, and may be used in funeral sermons.

Job 1:21; 19:25-27
Psalm 23
Isaiah 25:8; 26:19
Matthew 11:28
John 3:16; 11:25-26; 14:2, 27
1 Corinthians 2:9; 15:21-22, 54-55; 15:40
Revelation 20:12-13
Alma 11:42-44; 40:11-12
D&C 42:45

The Graveside Prayer

The graveside prayer is the concluding part of the funeral service, with the officiating leader continuing to conduct the service at the cemetery. He may appropriately give a brief message of hope and faith to the family prior to the prayer. He would then announce that the graveside service concludes the memorial for (name of the deceased), and announce the name of the person who is to offer the graveside prayer.

Generally a priesthood holder offers this dedicatory prayer; however, any friend chosen by the family is permitted to dedicate the grave, with or without priesthood authority. The following are suggestions for the graveside prayer.

1. The beginning might include these words: "Our Heavenly Father, we approach thee in prayer as we surround this area of earth which has been prepared to receive the body of _____ , and we dedicate this grave as a resting place for (his or her) mortal remains."

2. The body of the prayer should be a supplication on behalf of the family, with words of comfort and courage and counsel or blessings of which they might be in need. This is a very intimate moment and the person who offers the prayer should be under the influence of the Holy Ghost.

3. The conclusion might acknowledge that the site is a hallowed spot, with a request that it be protected from the elements and that family members and friends might come to the grave to receive consolation and inspiration as they reflect upon the life of the deceased. Then the prayer might include words similar to these: "We ask also that at the time appointed for (his or her) resurrection, the body of _____ will again come forth, reunited with the spirit." It should, of course, be concluded with the words "In the name of Jesus Christ. Amen."

Suggested Reading

Richard L. Evans, remarks at funeral of Elder John A. Widtsoe, in *Richard L. Evans—The Man and the Message*, Bookcraft, 1973, pp. 179-83. See also pp. 127, 163, 164, 292-94.

Heber J. Grant, "Death of My Last Son," in *Gospel Standards*, compiled by G. Homer Durham, Improvement Era Publication, 1969, pp. 364-66.

Marion D. Hanks, eulogy sermon of Elder Richard L. Evans in *The Gift of Self*, Bookcraft, 1974, pp. 159-65.

Spencer W. Kimball, "Tragedy or Destiny," *Faith Precedes the Miracle*, Deseret Book Co., 1972, pp. 95-106.

Harold B. Lee, "David O. McKay: He Lighted the Lamps of Faith," *Stand Ye in Holy Places*, Deseret Book Co., 1974, pp. 173-80. (Address delivered at funeral services for President David O. McKay.)

Harold B. Lee, *Ye Are the Light of the World*, Deseret Book Co., 1974: "If a Man Die, Shall He Live Again," pp. 225-43; "Faith to Surmount Life's Inevitables," pp. 246-50; "From the Valley of Despair to the Mountain Peaks of Hope," pp. 251-60.

Thomas S. Monson, *Pathways to Perfection*, Deseret Book Co., 1973, pp. 1-8, 164-65, 284-88.

Boyd K. Packer, *Teach Ye Diligently*, Deseret Book Co., 1975, pp. 230-37. Explanation especially for children concerning life, death, and the mission of Christ.

Joseph Smith, "The King Follett Discourse," in *Teachings of the Prophet Joseph Smith*, compiled by Joseph Fielding Smith, Deseret Book Co., 1938, pp. 342-62. See also pp. 196-210.

Joseph F. Smith, *Gospel Doctrine*, Deseret Book Co., 1939, pp. 277-78. See also "Eternal Life and Salvation," pp. 428-77.

CHAPTER 25

The Missionary Report

Every eye in the audience was on the returned missionary as he told of faith-promoting experiences of his mission. His stirring testimony rang firm and clear as church members vicariously experienced his missionary experiences and felt the impact of his words.

Aside from talks by General Authorities, there are few talks that can be more powerful and influential than the missionary report.

A young missionary nearing the end of his mission commented, "I'm already planning my welcome-home speech, because it is the perfect set-up for presenting a really great talk." He went on to describe special experiences that he was eager to share with family and friends at home.

Several factors contribute to making a welcome-home talk the "perfect set-up" for a church talk. A person who has just returned from a mission has completed a wonderful period in his life—fulltime service for the Lord. Because of the nature and importance of the work, he has had deep spiritual experiences and has forcefully felt the struggles between good and evil. For two years he has been an instrument for changing lives eternally. Most important, his own life has changed significantly. If a returned missionary has truly served a successful mission, he radiates the enthusiasm and sparkle of missionary work.

Family and friends have eagerly awaited his return. Young people are curious to see how he has changed. The stage is set and the audience is attentive. The returned missionary has center stage with the potential of greatly inspiring and motivating his listeners.

Thus we see the tremendous responsibility that rests upon a returned missionary as he reports his mission. Since he is expected to be a source of spiritual strength, listeners expect to hear spiritual highlights of his mission, to hear soul-touching and faith-promoting experiences. How disappointing is the report that is merely a travelogue or an inappropriate attempt to be humorous.

Careful preparation should be given to the missionary report.

Don'ts for the Missionary Report

1. Don't make your speech a travelogue or center it on humor.

2. Don't belittle the habits, customs, and people of other countries.

3. Don't try to provide earth-shaking stories by exaggerating the truth.

4. Don't try to say too much. There will be other opportunities to speak in firesides and youth groups.

Do's for the Missionary Report

1. Do have a speech outline.

2. Do use scriptures and personal stories.

3. Do present a brief gospel message from one of the missionary discussions with related scriptures, such as repentance, the Word of Wisdom, or tithing. This could be the heart of your talk.

4. Do discuss your personal preparations for a mission and suggestions for prospective missionaries.

5. Do bear testimony of how a mission has influenced your life.

Ironically, the best way to prepare for a missionary report talk is to prepare well for a mission. If one has adequately prepared physically and spiritually for his missionary work, he will have something to report when he returns. His mission will be filled with faith-promoting experiences, which will provide rich and stimulating material for his return-home report.

A chapter on a missionary report must include a consideration of how to prepare for a mission, for as distant chronologically as the two may seem, they are very closely related. A successful report can only come from a successful mission. President Joseph F. Smith once told a group of missionaries:

It is a wonderful responsibility that you bear. You are the heralds of salvation to mankind. The message which you bear must first be understood and observed by you in person, in order that you may the more effectively establish the Word in the hearts of others. You have no time to lose. Every moment should be occupied by study or by the proclamation of the word of God. (Liahona 13:424b.)

President Spencer W. Kimball has said that every young person should be prepared to fill a mission. Let's consider, therefore, some specific ways to prepare for a mission and thus prepare for an inspiring return-home talk. The following suggestions are a compilation of observations from mission presidents, bishops, parents of missionaries, returned missionaries, youth, and other Church leaders.

How to Prepare for a Mission

1. *Physical preparation.* Learn proper eating habits and nutrition. Learn how to cook nourishing and simple meals. Obey the Word of Wisdom and observe proper sleeping habits. Develop the habit of arising at six A.M. Strengthen your body by exercising each day.

2. *Moral preparation.* Live the commandments, especially keeping morally clean. Observe all standards of dress and grooming. Strive to be honest in all aspects of your daily living.

3. *Financial preparation.* Begin in your youth to save money for a mission. Learn how to budget your finances. Parents might start a savings account at a child's birth and then encourage the child to consistently add to it. If a two-year mission costs $3600, the parent might establish a savings plan of putting $8.35 into the account each month. In 19 years at 6 percent interest, the account will grow to $3,578. A teenager should also be encouraged to obtain a job to earn money for a mission.

146

4. *Intellectual preparation.* Improve reading skills by adopting a daily reading program. Expand your mental powers by memorizing scriptures and other quotations. Take a public speaking course so that you might be more effective in communicating. Learn a foreign language.

5. *Spiritual preparation.* Study the gospel regularly. Take a teacher development class and teach in Sunday School or Primary. Young men should also magnify their callings as home teachers; this is excellent preparation for talking about the gospel.

Perhaps the greatest way to prepare for a mission is to increase spirituality in the home. This puts a responsibility on parents and family of prospective missionaries to set good examples, and also challenges the missionary to encourage family prayer, morning and night, as well as family gospel study programs. The weekly family home evening provides great strength for prospective missionaries. Family pride and tradition should also be fostered in the home.

An outstanding example of how a missionary was trained through his family is the story of Lance Cooper of Fresno, California. Lance was a high school football star, was named to four all-star teams, and was selected as an All American player. He was offered many scholarships, and thirty-three colleges expressed an interest in him. But because of his desire to serve a mission, Lance declined all these offers. He said, "It's hard for many of my friends to understand why I would want to go on a mission and risk losing a scholarship, but I'm not worried. I figure that if I do what the Lord wants me to do, everything will work out for my best interests." He also stated, "If I can succeed also by playing for a major college, then maybe other boys who play football will say, 'Look at Lance. He went on a mission—maybe I can do both, too.' "

It is this kind of personal commitment that prepares the way for a successful and spiritual mission, resulting in an inspiring report at the end of missionary service.

Suggested Outline for a Missionary Report (20-30 minute talk)

I. Introduction
   A. Tell a story to introduce the gospel message theme

II. Body
  A. Gospel message—for example, repentance (part of one of the missionary discussions with related scriptures)
    1. Scriptures and ideas
    2. Examples relating this topic to missionary activities
    3. Stress the value of being familiar with the missionary discussions
  B. Brief background to familiarize audience with your mission (Choose one or two of these five options, and be brief)
    1. Your mission: geographical; one or two historical points; towns in which you labored
    2. Your mission president and his family and the influence they had on your life
    3. Your companions: two or three and their good qualities and what you learned from them
    4. Your daily schedule: a typical day's work from 6:30 A.M. to 10:30 P.M.
    5. Methods of proselyting: office calls, tracting, bus stops, referrals
  C. Missionary experiences
    1. Human interest stories of successes in converting
    2. Challenges of missionary work
    3. Other faith-promoting stories relevant to your mission
III. Conclusion
  A. Express sincere thanks to:
    1. God and his prophet for calling you
    2. Parents, family, bishop, and ward members for their support
    3. Any special group or individual who helped make your mission possible
  B. Evaluate your missionary preparation and make an application to prospective missionaries
  C. Bear testimony that you know that the Lord, through his prophet, called you to carry the restored gospel to his children in (the name of your mission)

CHAPTER 26

Stories That Illustrate

Stories can be used effectively in a church talk to hold the listeners' interest and attention and buttress points the speaker wishes to make. When you select a story, be certain that it pertains to your subject and reinforces your message. Stories are better if they can be retold, in your own words. If you must read them, practice them beforehand, so you can read smoothly and look up at the audience occasionally.

Good sources for inspirational stories are the church periodicals (*Ensign, New Era,* and *Friend*), the family home evening manual, other church books, as well as great secular literature. Here are some examples of stories that are quoted verbatim or are condensed, to illustrate particular subjects.

Subject: Christ

What It Means to Know Christ

To know the Lord is to know that we can pray through him and converse in prayer as one converses with another. In preparation for a special speaking engagement, I prayed to know what it meant to really know the Lord. The idea that came to my mind had a profound impact on me. It was a question: Whom do you really know in earth life?

As I thought about that idea, I decided that I knew my father quite well. So I then began thinking about the experiences that enabled me to really know my father. As I reflected, I remembered how as a young boy growing up on the farm, I spent many, many hours in conversation with my father. Even though many of the things I wanted to talk about were childish and trivial, Dad always listened carefully and encouraged me to talk to him. As the years slipped by, our conversations became deeper and more meaningful. A great joy of each day was talking to him, and I never looked forward to the end of a conversation. In fact, I would go out of my way for the privilege of talking to him for even a few minutes.

Following an institute convention in Provo, I drove to Idaho and spent two days visiting my parents. Just before leaving I walked out to the stockyard with my father and there expressed to him some concerns I had. He then shared a beautiful spiritual experience with me that greatly comforted me. After embracing my father I got in the car and headed for Colorado. As I drove away, I was impressed that, at least for our relationship, the reason Dad could share that choice, sacred experience with me was because we had, over the years, laid a foundation by many long hours of deeply intimate conversation.

Just a week later, while driving alone to a distant city in Wyoming, I lifted my voice in prayer to my Heavenly Father. Not many minutes slipped by when, under the influence of the Spirit, I walked, as it were, back through many beautiful experiences I had had with my earthly father. I felt of his love. His presence seemed close and real. I wept for joy as I realized how precious our relationship was.

The next morning while I was preparing for breakfast in the home of some good Saints, the phone rang. I was told that during the night my father had passed away. As I reflected on the experience of the night before, I realized that many choice experiences and conversations had developed a great bond of love between my father and myself. Thinking about this, I could see that the same principle was true relative to building a relationship with the Lord—the more we pray through him in prayer, the more we bring him and gospel principles into our lives, the closer is our relationship with him. I seemed to sense that the relationship we have with our earthly father is a symbol of the kind of relationship we

150

also may have with the Lord. (George W. Pace, "What It Means to Know Christ," *Ensign*, September 1974, p. 46.)

Subject: Youth
Dandy: An Impulsive Colt

Recently I had great pleasure in training a well-bred colt. He had a good disposition, clean, well-rounded eye, was well proportioned, and all in all, a choice equine possession. Under the saddle he was as willing, responsive, and co-operative as a horse could be. He and my dog Scotty were real companions. I liked the way he would go up to something of which he was afraid. He had confidence that if he would do as I bade him he would not be injured.

But Dandy resented restraint. He was ill-contented when tied and would nibble at the tie rope until he was free. He would not run away; he just wanted to be free. Thinking other horses felt the same, he would proceed to untie their ropes. He hated to be confined in the pasture, and if he could find a place in the fence where there was only smooth wire, he would paw the wire carefully with his feet until he could step over to freedom. More than once my neighbors were kind enough to put him back in the field. He learned even to push open the gate. Though his depredations were provoking and sometimes expensive, I admired his ingenuity.

But his curiosity and desire to explore the neighborhood led him and me into trouble. Once on the highway he was hit by an automobile, resulting in a demolished machine, injury to the horse, and slight, though not serious, injury to the driver.

Recovering from that, and still impelled by a feeling of wanderlust, he inspected the fence throughout the entire boundary. He even found the gates wired. So, for awhile we thought we had Dandy secure in the pasture.

One day, however, somebody left the gate unwired. Detecting this, Dandy unlatched it, took Nig, his companion, with him, and together they visited the neighbor's field. They went to an old house used for storage. Dandy's curiosity prompted him to push open the door. There was a sack of grain. What a find! Yes, and what a tragedy! The grain was poisoned bait for rodents! In a few minutes Dandy and Nig were in spasmodic pain, and shortly both were dead.

How like Dandy are many of our youth! They are not bad; they do not even intend to do wrong; but they are impulsive, full of life, full of curiosity, and long to do something. They, too, are restive under restraint, but if they are kept busy, guided carefully and rightly, they prove to be responsive and capable; but if left to wander unguided, they all too frequently find themselves in the environment of temptation and too often are entangled in the snares of evil. (David O. McKay, *Gospel Ideals*, pp. 518-19.)

Subject: Appreciation
I Found My Mother

Perhaps like most teenagers, I have taken my parents' love for granted. I never really considered the immeasurable amount of time, effort, money, or patience they spent on me. Particularly with my mother was this the case.

It seems, now, that many times I resented my mother, resented things she stood for, things she asked me to do, things she told me about her childhood life. I resented the fact that I, as the eldest of seven children, had all the responsibility; or so I felt. It was up to me to set the example—a word I grew to hate—to lead the way, to try things and get into trouble so that, it seemed, the way was clear for the other children to do just about what they would. I remember how I resented the certain tone of voice Mother used to call me to help her. Certain phrases stand out in my mind, and I can hear the tone even now:

"Kristy, help me with dinner."

"The twins need their shoes cleaned."

"Kristy, Sue and Gay are quarreling; can't you do something?"

"Nancy needs some attention; would you read her a story?"

I always felt like saying "No," but, of course, I didn't.

Then September came and I went away to school. All my younger life the school had carried with it a romantic aura to me. It was there my parents met; there they fell in love and were married; there I was born. So I anxiously looked forward to going—for me—"home."

152

But at that time, in September, there was more to it than that: I wanted to get away from home—my real home. And yet, as time passed and I read my mother's letters telling me about the day-to-day things she did, I began to realize, deep within me, that she gave all her time, money, effort, and thought to her children. I learned that all the meetings, all the shopping, all the housecleaning, all the teaching—actually everything—was directly or indirectly related to serving her family. And all this I learned so slowly and subtly that I barely realized the knowledge was there.

Then one day I came home from my morning classes and found a letter from my mother. It was a simple, ordinary letter, full of the news of home. It told how Dave and Dan, the twins, had flushed a whole roll of tissue paper down the toilet, which flooded over just as Mother was ready to leave for Relief Society. It told how Mother simply had to find the time to give Sandy a haircut. It told of Mother taking Nancy to dancing lessons, and watching her, and being so proud of her.

It was just a regular, everyday letter, but I had scarcely reached the second page when a feeling suddenly started within me and spread throughout me. It was like the sun bursting from behind a cloud, spreading its sunshine. I could all of a sudden see my mother as she really was—an unselfish, loving, and celestial being, the person who had done more for me than anyone else, and yet the person to whom I gave the least credit.

I threw myself on my bed and cried; cried with the gladness of the sudden discovery; cried with the unhappiness of my ingratitude, and how it had undoubtedly hurt my mother. I quickly wrote her a letter and told her of my love and appreciation for her. It wasn't a good letter, but it was a sincere one; and she wrote back just as quickly:

"Dearest Kristy, I read your letter, and I wept." (Kristine Walker, *New Era*, October 1974, p. 27.)

Subject: Goals
The Great Stone Face

"The Great Stone Face," by Nathaniel Hawthorne, is the story of a boy named Ernest who lived in the mountains of New

England. On the front of one of these mountains was a formation that looked like a human face revealed each night at sunset. It was a kind face, and Ernest thought it smiled down on him.

The people had a legend that someday a child would be born who would grow to be noble and great and whose face would resemble the face on the mountain. Ernest thought about this tradition and wondered if he would live to see that great man. Years passed and Ernest grew to manhood. After each day's work he would look at the face, which always gave him encouragement as he remembered what people had said. He could not do unkind things or think unkind thoughts while the Great Stone Face was looking down upon him.

Through the years a number of notable men came back to their home town, but Ernest could find in none of their faces the noble qualities he saw in the Great Stone Face.

Ernest became an old man. His neighbors had grown to love him and to seek his counsel. One day a poet visited him. He was a great man, and Ernest wondered if he would resemble the Great Stone Face. But no, his face lacked depth of character.

The poet and Ernest sat together as the last rays of the setting sun fell upon Ernest's face. The poet stared in wonder. Here was the man for whom they had been waiting—the man tradition had said would come. Ernest's face was the image of the Great Stone Face!

Ernest had become the man of the legend because he had made what he saw in the stone face his goal in life. He did not become wealthy, he did not become a great general, he did not become a great statesman. He became a man whom all admired, because he forgot himself in service. His goals were worthy, and his life was filled with goodness. (Adapted from Nathaniel Hawthorne, "The Great Stone Face," in the Relief Society Manual, 1973-74.)

Subject: Sabbath
The Standby Pitcher

David had been playing for a little league team all season. More than anything else he wanted to be a regular on the team, and he wanted to be a pitcher. He never missed a practice or a game. Whenever his dad or his older brother could find the time, he'd get them to play catch with him. Even when David watched television he would wear his baseball mitt and pop a ball in and out of it almost automatically. Sometimes he'd forget to take the mitt off when his mother called him for meals, and then the family would have to wait while David put the mitt away, washed his hands, and came to the table.

Near the end of the season the coach told all the little leaguers they should meet at the ball park on a certain Sunday morning to have a special practice and to have their pictures taken. "I can't come on Sunday," said David.

"You'd better," said the coach, "because we're going to talk about our team for next year after we have our pictures taken."

Usually, David ran home full of excitement after a ball game or a practice. But this night he was late, and he hardly answered when his family spoke to him. He was unusually quiet all week, but on Sunday he didn't go to the ball park. On Monday he was at practice and at every practice afterward. Finally the day came for the team tryouts.

"You'll be one of our regular pitchers," the coach told David, "but you'll have to play whenever a game is scheduled. We need you, and that will mean sometimes you will play on a Sunday."

"I can't play ball on Sundays," David said.

"Then you'll have to be a standby pitcher instead of a regular one," answered the coach. And that is how it was all season. Sometimes David had a chance to pitch a game but more often he didn't. The other boys on the team played on Sundays, but David went to Sunday School and sacrament meeting with his family.

In the spring when David was ten years old, the coach called the boys together to begin a new season and to make selections for the team. "We'll need you for a regular pitcher this year, David," he said. "But sometimes you'll need to play on Sunday."

"I'll have to think about it," said David. That night he talked the problem over with his dad, and then he said a special prayer for help to have the courage to do what he knew was right. The next day he told the coach he'd have to be just a standby pitcher again. The coach only shook his head.

Several weeks went by and David was at every practice. One night the coach called the boys around him. He explained that

155

David couldn't play ball on Sunday even though the team often had a game on that day. "But I'd like him to be our pitcher anyhow," he went on. "If you agree, we could let David be our regular weekday pitcher and have a standby pitcher for Sunday games. How about it?"

There was a moment of silence. David could hardly breathe. The team members hesitated for only a minute, and then every little leaguer agreed wholeheartedly to the Sunday standby pitcher plan. (*Friend,* February 1975, p. 40.)

Subject: Service
LDS Youth Wash Cars to Aid Nonmember Teen

A 16-year-old boy, injured in an automobile accident, lay unconscious in a hospital for five months. When he was taken home, he was in a state of semi-consciousness.

The accident, which was a tragedy for the teenager's family, was compounded by the fact that there was no automobile insurance to ease the financial burden of the enormous hospital bills.

The victim and his family are not members of the Church, but the Aaronic Priesthood and the Young Women of the Gridley California Stake haven't placed religious boundaries upon their love for others and their ability to care about their fellowmen.

They didn't know the boy but when they heard of his situation, they wanted to help. In the bishop's youth council meeting of the Gridley 1st Ward, the idea for a service project originated; the project plans were then presented to the stake youth council. Members of the council decided to conduct a car wash.

They planned the entire project, executing every detail, including the final presentation of the proceeds to the parents of the accident victim.

"When we walked into the room where the boy was, it was really sad to see someone our own age lying helpless and unable to speak," said Denise Skousen, secretary to the stake youth council. "It made us sorry that we couldn't have done more to help."

Lynn Barrow, a Laurel president, said, "It gave me a neat feeling and it was fun doing something for someone who needed it."

Robert McDowell, an Explorer president, first approached the boy's father to get permission to conduct the car wash. "He was quite skeptical because of the total youth involvement," Robert said. "But he did agree to let us go ahead with the project."

The parents were overwhelmed when a stake youth committee presented them with $376.

The mother asked each member of the committee where they were from, and expressed surprise that the youth would put forth so much effort to help someone they didn't know. "You're really something special," was the grateful mother's response.

The father said, "I admit that when Bob approached me about the project, I really didn't believe anything would ever come of it. This has really been one of the nicest things that has ever happened to us. I am really impressed with these youth." (*Church News*, January 25, 1975, p. 11.)

Subject: Atonement
Saved From Drowning

President David O. McKay used to tell this story of a group of small boys just learning to swim. A short distance down the stream was a deep, treacherous hole. One of the boys somehow fell into the hole. He was helpless to save himself and, for a moment, the other boys did not know what to do to help him. Then one boy with presence of mind jerked a long stick from a willow fence and held one end of it toward the drowning boy. By grasping it and holding on tightly, the boy was saved.

All the boys said the one who nearly drowned owed his life to the boy who furnished the means of rescue. And this is true. He could never have saved himself, but the stick alone could not have saved him either. The drowning boy had to put forth all his strength to reach the stick and hang on. . . . Christ is like the rescuer and his atonement is like the stick. Christ offers us the atonement as the way to receive forgiveness. When we repent we reach out to accept the atonement, just as the drowning boy reached out to accept the stick. If we accept the atonement by repenting we will be forgiven and not have to continue suffering for our sins. (*Family Home Evenings*, 1974-1975, p. 89.)

Subject: Inactivity
Is Dependence on Christ Necessary for You?

A certain quorum president had persistently visited an inactive quorum member to encourage him to more activity and faithfulness to his duty. One evening the quorum president came to visit the inactive elder. As they visited before a warm, pleasant fire in the living room, the quorum president attempted to persuade the elder to activity. "Frankly, Jim" said the elder, "I really haven't felt the need for the Church. I still believe in Christ, and I believe the Church is true, but I don't see how my being present every Sunday is that essential—I seem to be getting along quite well by myself."

After some discussion, the quorum president arose and went to the fire place, and with the poker, stroked out a red hot coal on the hearth of the fireplace. Both the elder and president watched as the coal gradually cooled and the red glow of the burning coal became ashen white. The elder then spoke: "I get your point, Jim. Don't say it. I'll be there next Sunday." (*When Thou Art Converted, Strengthen Thy Brethren*, 1974-1975 Course of Study for the Melchizedek Priesthood, p. 86.)

Steps to
Successful Speaking

Be diligent in preparation. Obtain spiritual guidance through prayer.

Select a stimulating subject that sparks interest in you and your audience.

Rehearse your speech aloud.

Your introduction must gain the audience's attention. Never apologize. Be positive, confident.

Be interesting, convincing, enthusiastic. Speak clearly. Maintain eye contact with the audience.

Illustrate your ideas with quotations, stories, examples.

Watch the audience for feedback on their attention, interest.

Conclude on time with a brief, direct summary.

Practice what you preach—be a good example always in your own life.

Following these steps will lead to a successful experience for both speaker and audience!

Bibliography

Arnold, Carroll C., Douglas Ehninger, and John C. Gerber. *The Speaker's Resource Book.* Chicago: Scott, Foresman & Co., 1966.

Ballard, Melvin R. *Melvin J. Ballard, Crusader for Righteousness.* Salt Lake City: Bookcraft, 1966.

Bartlett, John. *Familiar Quotations.* 13th ed. Boston: Little, Brown & Co., 1955.

Berry, Thomas Elliott, *The Most Common Mistakes in the English Usage.* Philadelphia: Chilton Book Co., 1961.

Blackwood, Andrew Watterson. *The Preparation of Sermons.* New York: Abingdon Press, 1968.

Borden, Richard C. *Public Speaking as Listeners Like It.* New York: Harper & Row Publishers, Inc., 1935.

Bradley, John P., Leo F. Daniels, and Thomas C. Jones. *The International Dictionary of Thoughts.* Chicago: J. G. Ferguson Publishing Co., 1969.

Brigance, William N. *A History and Criticism of American Public Address.* Vols. I & II. New York: Russell & Russell, 1960.

Crocker, Lionel. *Public Speaking for College Students.* New York: American Book Co., 1956.

Doxey, Roy W. *The Word of Wisdom Today.* Salt Lake City: Deseret Book Co., 1975.

Edwards, Tryon, comp. *The New Dictionary of Thoughts.* Standard Book Co., 1961.

Evans, Richard L., Jr. *Richard L. Evans, The Man and the Message.* Salt Lake City: Bookcraft, 1973.

Garff, Royal L. *You Can Learn to Speak.* Salt Lake City: Wheelwright Lithographing Co., 1950.

Grant, Heber J. *Gospel Standards.* Compiled by G. Homer Durham. Salt Lake City: Improvement Era, 1941.

Green, Forace, comp. *Testimonies of Our Leaders.* Salt Lake City: Bookcraft, 1958.

Hanks, Marion D. *The Gift of Self.* Salt Lake City: Bookcraft, 1974.

Hayakawa, S.I. *Language in Thought.* New York: Harcourt Brace & Co., 1941.

Heslop, J M., and Dell R. Van Orden. *From the Shadow of Death.* Salt Lake City: Deseret Book Co., 1973.

Hochmuth, Marie K. *A History and Criticism of American Public Address.* Vol. III. New York: Longman, Green & Co., 1955.

Hymns. Salt Lake City: The Church of Jesus Christ of Latter-day Saints, 1958.

Kimball, Spencer W. *Faith Precedes the Miracle.* Salt Lake City: Deseret Book Co., 1972.

Knott, H.E. *How to Prepare a Sermon.* Cincinnati: Standard Publishing Foundation, 1963.

Lee, Harold B. *Ye Are the Light of the World.* Salt Lake City: Deseret Book Co., 1974.

Lloyd-Jones, D. Martyn. *Preaching and Preachers.* Grand Rapids: Zondervan Publishing House, 1971.

Lomas, Charles W., and Ralph Richardson. *Speech—Idea and Delivery.* Boston: Houghton Mifflin Co., 1963.

McBurney, James H., and Ernest J. Wrage. *Guide to Good Speech.* Englewood Cliffs, N.J.: Prentice-Hall, Inc., 1965.

McConkie, Bruce R. *Mormon Doctrine.* Salt Lake City: Bookcraft, 1966.

McFarland, Kenneth. *Eloquence in Public Speaking.* Englewood Cliffs, N.J.: Prentice-Hall, Inc., 1961.

McKay, David O. *Gospel Ideals.* Salt Lake City: Improvement Era, 1953.

Monson, Thomas S. *Pathways to Perfection.* Salt Lake City: Deseret Book Co., 1973.

Monroe, Alan H., and Douglas Ehninger. *Principles of Speech*. Chicago: Scott, Foresman & Co., 1964.

Nelson, N.L. *Preaching and Public Speaking among Latter-day Saints*. 2nd ed. Salt Lake City: The Deseret News, 1910.

Packer, Boyd K. *Teach Ye Diligently*. Salt Lake City: Deseret Book Co., 1975.

Smith, Joseph Fielding. *Doctrines of Salvation*. Vol. II. Compiled by Bruce R. McConkie. Salt Lake City: Bookcraft, 1955.

Smith, Joseph F. *Gospel Doctrine*. Salt Lake City: Deseret Book Co., 1939.

Smith, Joseph. *Teachings of the Prophet Joseph Smith*. Compiled by Joseph Fielding Smith. Salt Lake City: Deseret Book Co., 1938.

Talmage, James E. *Jesus the Christ*. 32nd ed. Salt Lake City: Deseret Book Co., 1962.

Tizard, Leslie J. *Preaching*. New York: Oxford University Press, 1958.

Walter, Otis M., and Robert L. Scott. *Thinking and Speaking*. New York: The Macmillan Co., 1962.

West, Emerson R. "A Study of the Reactions of Latter-day Saint Youth to the Thirteen Fireside Programs Given in the Winter of 1960." Unpublished Thesis, 1961.

West, Emerson R. *Profiles of the Presidents*. Salt Lake City: Deseret Book Co., 1972.

West, Emerson R., comp. *Vital Quotations*. Salt Lake City: Bookcraft, 1968.

West, Roy A. *Family Eternal*. Salt Lake City: Bookcraft, 1946.

Widtsoe, John A. *In a Sunlit Land*. Salt Lake City: Deseret Book Co., 1953.

The Bible, The Book of Mormon, and The Doctrine and Covenants, published by The Church of Jesus Christ of Latter-day Saints.

PERIODICALS AND MISCELLANEOUS

Church News, section of the *Deseret News*.

Conference Reports. Official Proceedings of the Annual and Semiannual Conferences of The Church of Jesus Christ of Latter-day Saints.

The Ensign.

The Family Home Evening Manual.

The Friend.

The Improvement Era.

The Instructor.

Liahona.

Melchizedek Priesthood Quorum Study Guide, 1974-75.

MIA Speech Director's Guide and Workbook, The Church of Jesus Christ of Latter-day Saints, 1965-74.

The New Era.

The Relief Society Magazine.

Relief Society Course of Study, 1973-74.

Index

165